mathematical
puzzles
of

Selected and Edited by Martin Gardner

Dover Publications, Inc., New York

Published in Canada by General Publishing Company, Ltd., 30 Lesmill Road, Don Mills, Toronto,
Ontario.
Published in the United Kingdom by Constable
and Company, Ltd., 10 Orange Street, London WC 2.

This Dover edition, first published in 1959 under
the title *Mathematical Puzzles of Sam Loyd*, Volume
I, is a new selection of puzzles from the *Cyclopedia
of Puzzles*, which was privately published in 1914
by Samuel Loyd, Jr. Martin Gardner selected the
puzzles and edited the text of this Dover edition.

International Standard Book Number: 0-486-20498-7
Library of Congress Catalog Card Number: 58-14139

Manufactured in the United States of America
Dover Publications, Inc.
180 Varick Street
New York, N.Y. 10014

CLASSIFIED TABLE OF CONTENTS

Arithmetic and Algebraic Problems

Probability and Game Theory Problems

Operations Research Problems

Plane Geometry Problems

Geometrical Dissection Problems

Route, Tracing, and Topological Problems

Counter and Sliding Block Problems

Solid Geometry Problems

INTRODUCTION

Samuel Loyd, America's greatest puzzlist, was born in Philadelphia on January 30, 1841. Three years later his father, a wealthy real estate operator, settled in New York where young Sam attended public school until he was seventeen. He was a tall, slim, quiet spoken individualist; skilled in such curious arts as conjuring, mimicry, ventriloquism, chess playing, and the rapid cutting of silhouettes from sheets of black paper. Early plans for a career in civil engineering evaporated as his interest grew in the game of chess.

Bertrand Russell once remarked that at the age of eighteen he was so passionately fond of chess that he forced himself to stop playing on the grounds that unless he did so he would do nothing else. Had Loyd made a similar decision he might have achieved eminence as an engineer; but then the world would have been poorer in another respect, for recreational mathematics (which may be said to include chess as well as mathematical puzzles) is a form of intellectual play, and who can say that play is any less essential to the good life than guided missiles and atomic bombs?

Sam learned to play a fair game of chess at the age of ten. At fourteen, his first chess problem was published in the *New York Saturday Courier,* April 14, 1855, and within a few years he was recognized as the nation's foremost composer of chess puzzles. In those days there was an enormous popular interest in chess and scores of newspapers carried regular chess columns which printed problems sent in by readers. Loyd contributed to most of them, winning prize after prize for his ingenious, off-trail ideas. In 1857, when he was sixteen, he became problem editor of the *Chess Monthly*, then edited by Paul Morphy and D. W. Fiske. (Fiske often dressed up Loyd's problems with unusual tales and anecdotes, a technique that Loyd later used with great effectiveness in the presentation of his mathematical puzzles.) In subsequent years Loyd edited other chess columns for newspapers and magazines, including a weekly chess page that ran for a time in the *Scientific American Supplement*. He was usually his own best contributor, often hiding his identity behind such pseudonyms as W. King, A. Knight, and W. K. Bishop.

Although Loyd agreed that the best problems should be of a type possible in actual play, his virtuosity frequently found an outlet in problems that can only be described as fantastic. Almost every conceivable gimmick was exploited: solutions hinging upon *en passant* moves, a mate in "half a move" that called for the completion of castling, problems in which you retracted a move before mating, or forced a mate upon yourself, or mated with your opponent's help. He delighted in problems in which the pieces formed peculiar geometric designs on the board, numerals, letters, or even pictures of animals and objects. Chess playing friends often received from Loyd a birthday card bearing a chess problem that formed their own initials or monogram!

In one of his columns Loyd once announced that he had discovered a method by which a knight and two rooks could mate a lone king in the middle of the board! Readers were at first furious, then very much amused when Loyd finally disclosed his preposterous solution:

Unfortunately, Loyd did not excel in tournament chess, though he occasionally won a game with brilliant combination play. During a Paris tournament in 1867 he announced a mate in eight moves, and after explaining it carefully, his opponent resigned. Later it was discovered that not only did the opponent have an "out," he actually stood an excellent chance to win! The judges allowed Loyd to keep the game, however, on the grounds that his opponent had accepted the pseudo-mate.

After 1870 Loyd's interest in chess began to wane and he turned his attention toward mathematical puzzles and novelty advertising give-aways, tackling them with a zest and originality that has never been surpassed. In his youth he had devised a cardboard cut-out puzzle called "The Trick Donkeys" that had been enormously profitable. P. T. Barnum distributed millions of them, and young Loyd was said to have earned many thousands of dollars in a few weeks. Now he began to concentrate more and more on similar puzzles of wide general interest and commercial value. His 14-15 puzzle (see No. 21 of this collection) was a national craze both in the United States and abroad. His "Horse of Another Color" (See No. 45) also sold by the millions, as well as a simple mechanical puzzle involving steel balls under glass that bore the title of "Pigs in Clover." Many of his cardboard puzzles were printed by himself on a press which he owned in Elizabeth, New Jersey.

One of today's most popular advertising novelties is another Loyd creation — a pencil with a small loop of string at one end. You attach it a certain way to the victim's lapel buttonhole and he finds it extremely difficult to remove. Parcheesi, Loyd's adaptation of a traditional Indian board game of the same name, is still popular in the United States. The story of the game's origin is interesting. A business concern called Loyd one day to say they had bought a large supply of colored cardboard squares which they wanted to use for some type of game that could be sold on the street for a small price. Loyd expended so little effort in working out the game that he refused to charge for it, but the firm insisted on paying him ten dollars for his time. That was all he ever received, though the game later brought enormous profits to its various manufacturers.

In 1896 Loyd patented the most remarkable of his mechanical inventions — his famous "Get off the Earth" puzzle. Thirteen Chinese warriors appear around the rim of a rotating cardboard circle. By twisting the circle slightly, one warrior is made to vanish. Which warrior vanished and where did he go? Millions of this item were distributed as advertising give-aways in 1896. The following year another million (of a variation called "The Lost Jap") were handed out by the Metropolitan Life Insurance Company, with twenty prizes ranging from five to one hundred dollars for the best explanations received during a year's period. A still later modification, "Teddy and the Lions," was issued by Loyd in 1906.

During the 1890's Loyd wrote a popular column on puzzles for the *Brooklyn Daily Eagle,* and from the turn of the century until his death in 1911, his puzzle columns appeared in numerous newspapers and magazines. His monthly puzzle page in the *Woman's Home Companion* ran from 1904 until 1911.

When Loyd died on April 10, 1911, his son Samuel Loyd Jr. continued to edit his father's puzzle columns under the name of Sam Loyd. During his lifetime, Loyd senior had published only one hard-cover book, *Chess Strategy,* which he printed himself in 1878 on his New Jersey press. But after his death his son issued a number of collections of his father's puzzles, the most comprehensive of which was a mammoth *Cyclopedia of Puzzles,* privately published in 1914. The *Cyclopedia* was a hastily thrown together job, swarming with mistakes, omitted answers and typographical errors, nevertheless it remains today the largest, most exciting collection of puzzles ever assembled between the covers of one volume.

It is from this fabulous, long out of print tome that all the remarkable puzzles to follow have been taken. It is not known who provided the line drawings, but the text of the original *Cyclopedia* is in most cases a verbatim reprint from earlier newspaper and magazine columns by Loyd senior. For this collection the text has been edited for accuracy and clarity, but in such a way as to preserve the style and historical flavor of the original. To some of the problems I have added bracketed comments.

Many of the puzzles in Loyd's *Cyclopedia* are similar to puzzles that appear in the books of Henry Ernest Dudeney (1857-

1931), the famous British puzzle expert. In some cases it is possible to say with certainty that Dudeney borrowed from Loyd; in other cases, that Loyd borrowed from Dudeney. The task of tracing individual puzzles to their first publication by either man is so formidable, however, that one hesitates to say which expert took the most from the other. There was considerable rivalry between the two puzzlists while they were both active (only once in the entire *Cyclopedia* is Dudeney's name mentioned), and apparently each did not hesitate to appropriate and modify the other's inventions. In addition, both men drew heavily on common sources — traditional puzzles to which they gave new twists, and new puzzles of anonymous origin that passed from person to person in the manner of new jokes and limericks.

The puzzles reprinted here are only a portion of those contained in the *Cyclopedia*. I have limited the selection to mathematical puzzles (the *Cyclopedia* also contains thousands of riddles and word puzzles), choosing them with an eye both to variety and contemporary interest. If the book is well received, perhaps it will be followed by another selection from the same source.

Martin Gardner

1 *Where can you place another first magnitude star?*

THIS ODD puzzle is built upon the recent claim of a French astronomer to have located a new star of first magnitude. He says that the popular impression held by scientists of there being no more such stars is based entirely upon the discovery by a clever little puzzlist that the letters A-S-T-R-O-N-O-M-E-R-S form the pretty anagram "no more stars." We may mention that a still more appropriate anagram can be made with the same eleven letters.

The sketch shows the learned professor describing his new discovery to his brother astronomers. He has drawn the location of fifteen stars of different magnitudes, and is now going to show the position in the firmament of his new discovery.

See if you can draw the form of a five-pointed star which will be as large as any of the others and yet not touch one of them!

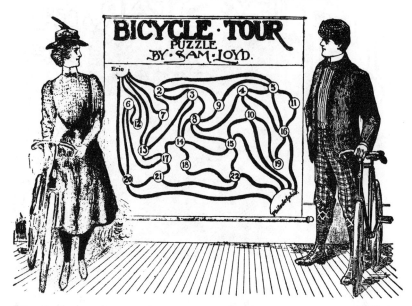

2 *Show the route from Philadelphia to Erie, passing once through all the towns.*

THE MAP shows twenty-three prominent cities of Pennsylvania connected by bicycle routes of more or less artistic design. The problem is a simple one: start on your summer outing and go from Philadelphia to Erie, passing once through every one of the cities and without going over any road twice. That is all there is to it.

The cities are numbered to enable solvers to describe their routes by a sequence of figures. In this trip the usual practice of getting there by the "shortest route possible," will be dispensed with. Just get there, without minding the cyclometer.

3 *Two Turkeys*

"TOGETHER THESE two turkeys weigh twenty pounds," said the butcher. "The little fellow sells for two cents a pound more than the big bird."

Mrs. Smith bought the little one for 82 cents and Mrs. Brown paid $2.96 cents for the big turkey. How much did each gobbler weigh?

4 Exchange the black and white pegs in the fewest number of moves.

I TAKE occasion to call attention to the origin of a pretty puzzle game, or species of solitaire, which became quite popular in Europe. It is an English invention, in that it was originated by an English sailor who spent forty years of his life at Sailor's Snug Harbor, on Staten Island, and whose proud boast was that he had sailed under Captain Randall, the founder of the institution.

The old sailor used to pick up quite a little bit of extra "baccy silver," as he termed it, by selling the puzzles to visitors as fast as he could whittle them out with a jack-knife. The game was brought out in London and enjoyed quite a run under the name of the English Sixteen Puzzle, but was never marketed on this side of the pond.

The object of the puzzle is to transpose the positions of the black and white pegs in the fewest number of moves. A peg may be moved from one square to an adjacent vacant square, or it may be jumped over an adjacent peg (of either color) provided it lands on a vacant square. Only moves along the rows (like a rook in chess) are permitted; no diagonal moves as in checkers.

According to an eye witness, the old sailor was very proud of his expertness, and used to give purchasers a rule to perform the feat in the fewest number of plays. He was mistaken, however, in his rule, or it must be classed along with the lost arts. Perhaps the world has advanced since his time, for the methods given in English puzzle books, as well as mathematical works, to be the shortest, are defective and may be shortened by several moves.

5 *Carnival Dice Game*

THE FOLLOWING dice game is very popular at fairs and carnivals, but since two persons seldom agree on the chances of a player winning, I offer it as an elementary problem in the theory of probability.

On the counter are six squares marked 1, 2, 3, 4, 5, 6. Players are invited to place as much money as they wish on any one square. Three dice are then thrown. If your number appears on one die only, you get your money back plus the same amount. If two dice show your number, you get your money back plus twice the amount you placed on the square. If your number appears on all three dice, you get your money back plus three times the amount. Of course if the number is not on any of the dice, the operator gets your money.

To make this clearer with an example, suppose that you bet $1 on No. 6. If one die shows a 6, you get your dollar back plus another dollar. If two dice show 6, you get back your dollar plus two dollars. If three dice show 6, you get your dollar back plus three dollars.

A player might reason: the chance of my number showing on one die is 1/6, but since there are three dice, the chances must be 3/6 or 1/2, therefore the game is a fair one. Of course this is the way the operator of the game wants everyone to reason, for it is quite fallacious.

Is the game favorable to the operator or the player, and in either case, just how favorable is it?

6 *With two straight cuts divide the horseshoe into seven pieces, one nail hole in each piece.*

HERE IS a puzzle based on the goblin story of "The Golden Horseshoe." This story tells how a gold horseshoe was cut into seven pieces, a nail hole in each piece, by two strokes of a sword, and how the seven pieces were then suspended by ribbons around the necks of seven children, as lucky talismans.

It is assumed that after the first cut the pieces may be piled up before giving the second blow, but the cuts must be straight and there must be no folding or bending of the paper. I showed the puzzle to a clever little jockey at a recent horse show. He made a paper horseshoe, and with the first cut divided it into three pieces; then by laying them together his second cut produced six pieces. The trick, however, is to get the seventh piece, and although it is really a simple puzzle it is sufficiently interesting to call for some study.

After you have solved the puzzle as stated, you are invited to try a second and more difficult problem. What is the largest number of pieces that can be produced by two cuts? The conditions are the same as before except that the nail holes may be disregarded.

7 *Martha's Vineyard*

IN COLONIAL days one of the sturdy settlers who had undertaken the difficult task of cultivating the rocky soil of an island off the coast of New England, essayed with the aid of his little daughter Martha, to set out a vineyard. To encourage her, as well as in lieu of other remuneration, he permitted Martha to cultivate for her own use a little square patch containing exactly a sixteenth of an acre of land.

It is said that she planted her vines according to custom, in rows nine feet apart, and cultivated them just like the others, yet, as the story goes, her little venture prospered and grew in a way that made Martha's Vineyard noted. She raised more grapes to the acre than any vineyard on the island and produced many new and valuable varieties.

That is all there is to the story when it is reduced to plain facts. Nevertheless, without wishing to impeach Martha's skill nor question her sweetness which imparted the flavor to her grapes, I wish to engraft a practical problem on her vines which may explain the reason for her wonderful success.

How many grape vines, not closer than nine feet apart, can be set out in a square plot one-sixteenth of an acre in size?

The problem is a pretty one, well calculated to tax the ingenuity of our mathematicians, but not to compel a return to the long forgotten school books, occasion is taken to say that an acre is 208 feet and 710/1000 of a foot square, so that a sixteenth of an acre is 52 feet 2 inches square. This you will observe is somewhat different from the popular measurement which prevails in rural districts, where a plot 210 feet square is reckoned an acre.

8 *Draw the Greek symbol with a continuous line, making the fewest possible turns.*

IN LOOKING over some photographs of marvelous relics of ancient times unearthed during the recent excavations in Greece, I was struck by the repeated appearance of the symbol of the circle and triangle. Not entering into the discussion regarding the accepted interpretation of the sign about which many volumes have been written by men of learning, I will merely call attention to the curious mathematical or puzzle feature which always appears to be a part of the scheme in such matters.

The sign is attached to certain inscriptions on memorial monuments somewhat in the nature of a seal or signature. It is pleasing to discover that the symbol can be drawn in one continuous line, without going over any line twice. But if we adopt the more popular plan of going over the same lines as often as one wishes, and merely require that the figure be drawn in one continuous line, making the fewest possible number of turns, it becomes by long odds the best puzzle of its kind ever produced.

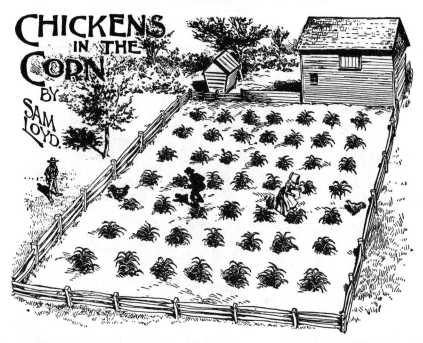

9 *Show the farmer and his wife how to catch the chickens.*

IN WATCHING the gambols of playful dogs, kittens, and other domestic animals we are often impressed by the way they seem to enter into the spirit of the fun and enjoy the fine points of play, just as human beings do. But for a rollicking exhibition of mischief, or "tantalizing cussedness" as the farmer calls it, I have never seen anything equal to the sport produced by two obstinate chickens refusing to be driven or coaxed from a garden. They neither fly nor run, but just dodge about, keeping close to their pursuers but always just out of reach. In fact, when the would-be captors retreat, the chickens become pursuers and follow close upon their heels, uttering sounds of defiance and contempt.

On a New Jersey farm, where some city folks were wont to summer, chicken-chasing became an everyday sport, and there were two pet chickens which could always be found in the garden ready to challenge any one to catch them. It reminded one of a game of tag, and suggested a curious puzzle which I am satisfied will worry some of our experts.

The object is to prove in just how many moves the good farmer and his wife can catch the two chickens. The field is divided into sixty-four square patches, marked off by the corn hills. Let us suppose that they are playing a game, moving between the corn rows from one square to another, directly up and down or right and left.

Play turn about. First let the man and woman each move one square, then let each of the chickens make a move. The play continues by turns until you find out in how many moves it is possible to drive the chickens into such positions that both of them are cornered and captured. A capture occurs when the farmer or his wife can pounce on a square occupied by a chicken.

The game can be played on any checkerboard by using two checkers of one color to represent the farmer and his wife, and two checkers of another color to represent the hen and rooster.

10 *Bixley To Quixley*

HERE IS a pretty problem which I figured out during a ride from Bixley to Quixley astride a razor-back mule. I asked Don Pedro, a native guide who walked ahead of me pulling the mule forward by its reins, if my steed had another gait. He said it had but that it was much slower, so I pursued my journey at uniform speed. To encourage Don Pedro, who was my chief propelling power, I said we would pass through Pixley, so as to get some liquid refreshments; and from that moment he could think of nothing but Pixley.

After we had been traveling for forty minutes I asked how far we had gone. Don Pedro replied: "Just half as far as it is to Pixley."

After creeping along for seven miles more I asked: "How far is it to Quixley?" He replied as before: "Just half as far as it is to Pixley."

We arrived at Quixley in another hour, which induces me to ask you to determine the distance from Bixley to Quixley.

THE SEDAN CHAIR PUZZLE

11 *Close the sedan chair by cutting it into the smallest number of pieces.*

"SPEAKING ABOUT modes of conveyance in China," says a writer who has spent most of his life in the Flowery Kingdom, "one soon gets used to being carried around in a sedan chair, which is far more comfortable and expeditious than a hack. These chairs are made of rattan wicker and remind you very much of those little Chinese puzzle boxes made of colored straws and so cleverly put together that you cannot discover where they are joined."

All this is suggestive of a clever puzzle, for those sedan chairs will close up to make a covered box when it rains, yet the closest examination will not detect where the pieces are joined. To illustrate the puzzle, you are asked to cut the chair into the fewest possible pieces which will fit together and form a perfect square.

12 How much does the storekeeper lose?

THE HEMP or manila rope trade, the most important industry of the Philippine islands, is controlled to a great extent by Chinese exporters who ship these products to all parts of the world. The traders and small dealers are Japanese who have an original way of doing business, peculiarly their own. The lack of established currency or fixed prices necessitates a wrangle over every transaction.

The accompanying puzzle sketch shows the ordinary way of doing business. Omitting the vernacular, we will say a Chinese sailor man saunters into a rope store and asks, "Can you direct me to a respectable shop where they sell good rope?"

The Japanese shopkeeper, swallowing the implied insult, says: "I keep only the best, but my poorest is probably better than what you want."

"Show me the best you have. It may serve until I find better. How much you ask for the cable rope?"

"Seven dollars the hank, one hundred feet long."

"Too long rope and too much money. I never pay more than one dollar for good, and this is rotten."

"Standard rope," replies the storekeeper, showing the unbroken seal which guarantees the length and quality. "If you have but little money, take what you want for two cents a foot."

"Cut off twenty feet," says the sailor, as he ostentatiously displays a five-dollar gold piece to show that he can pay. The storekeeper measures off twenty feet with an exaggerated display of anxiety to give full measure. The sailor notices, however, that the yardstick is just three inches shy, having been cut off at the 33-inch mark. So when the rope was cut he coolly points to the long end and says: "I take the eighty-foot piece. No, you need not send it. I carry it myself." Then he throws down the counterfeit five-dollar piece, which the storekeeper gets changed next door. As soon as the sailor gets his change he walks off with the rope.

The puzzle is to tell how much the storekeeper has lost, assuming that he is called upon to make good the counterfeit five-dollar gold piece and that the rope was really worth two cents a foot.

13 What Was The Profit?

A DEALER sold a bicycle for $50, then bought it back for $40, thereby clearly making $10 because he had the same bicycle back and $10 besides. Now having bought it for $40, he resold it for $45, and made $5 more, or $15 in all.

"But," says a bookkeeper, "the man starts off with a wheel worth $50, and at the end of the second sale has just $55! How then could he make more than $5? You see the selling of the wheel at $50 is a mere exchange which shows neither profit nor loss, but when he buys at $40 and sells at $45, he makes $5, and that is all there is to it."

"I claim," says an accountant, "that when he sells at $50 and buys back at $40, he has clearly and positively made $10, because he has the same wheel and $10, but when he now sells at $45 he makes that mere exchange referred to, which shows neither profit nor loss. This does not affect his first profit so he has made exactly $10."

It is a simple transaction which any scholar in the primary class should be able to figure out mentally, yet we are confronted by three different answers! Which in your opinion is right?

THE GRINDSTONE PUZZLE —BY— Sam Loyd

14 *How large was the grindstone when given to the second man?*

IT IS told that two honest Syrians pooled their savings and bought a grindstone. Because they lived several miles apart, they agreed that the elder man should keep the grindstone until he had reduced it in size by just one-half, then it should be turned over to the other.

The grindstone was exactly 22 inches in diameter, with a 3 and 1/7 inch hole in the center for the shaft, as shown in the picture. What would be the diameter of the stone when given to the second owner?

15 *The Bargain Sale*

IN DESCRIBING his experiences at a bargain sale, Smith says that half his money was gone in just thirty minutes, so that he was left with as many pennies as he had dollars before, and but half as many dollars as before he had pennies. Now, how much did he spend?

16 *Will the cat or dog win the race?*

MANY YEARS ago, when Barnum's Circus was of a truth "the greatest show on earth," the famous showman got me to prepare for him a series of prize puzzles for advertising purposes. They became widely known as the Questions of the Sphinx, on account of the large prizes offered to any one who could master them.

Barnum was particularly pleased with the problem of the cat and dog race, letting it be known far and wide that on a certain first day of April he would give the answer and award the prizes, or, as he aptly put it, "let the cat out of the bag, for the benefit of those most concerned."

The wording of the puzzle was as follows:

"A trained cat and dog run a race, one hundred feet straightaway and return. The dog leaps three feet at each bound and the cat but two, but then she makes three leaps to his two. Now, under those circumstances, what are the possible outcomes of the race?"

The fact that the answer was to be made public on the first of April, and the sly reference to "letting the cat out of the bag," was enough to intimate that the great showman had some funny answer up his sleeve.

17 *Arrange the ten pieces so that the snake will bite its tail.*

PROFESSOR VON SCHAFSKOPFEN, the distinguished naturalist, has been greatly exercised by conflicting stories concerning the Hoop Snake, so called on account of its peculiar mode of locomotion, produced by taking the end of its tail in its mouth and rolling along the ground like a hoop. This trait of the genus *ophidia* is described by many naturalists, and one college professor claims to have seen three snakes, combined in one large hoop, rolling along at lightning speed, then suddenly disappear by swallowing each other.

No one questions the possibility of the swallowing trick, but grave doubts have been thrown on the existence of the hoop snake. Professor Von Schafskopfen, scouring the country in search of specimens, finally discovered in the wilds of the Hoop Mountains a fine specimen of a petrified hoop snake with its tail in its mouth. With a fine saw he cut the snake into ten pieces, and, packing them in cotton, returned in triumph with his prize. Since then, unfortunately, he has been completely baffled in his attempts to readjust the pieces to make both ends meet.

Mathematicians say that the ten pieces can be arranged to make 362,882 different snakes without producing an endless hoop, which the sceptics claim goes to prove that it is 362,882 to 1 that no such snake ever existed!

THE **PLUMBER'S PROBLEM** BY SAM LOYD

18   *What is the most economical form of a tank designed to hold 1,000 cubic feet?*

HERE IS a practical plumbing lesson which will interest those of a mechanical turn of mind. Plumbers, boilermakers and tank builders estimate in cubic feet, reckoning seven and a half gallons to the cubic foot, which is close enough for all practical purposes. Of course a mathematician would tell us that there are 1,728 cubic inches to a cubic foot, because $12 \times 12 \times 12 = 1,728$, while to seven and one-half gallons there are $1,732\frac{1}{2}$ cubic inches, but then plumbers are a liberal set of fellows who cheerfully throw in the extra four and a half inches.

A plumber wanted to estimate the lowest possible cost of a copper tank to hold 1,000 cubic feet. Copper comes in sheets three feet square, worth $1.00 per square foot, so the problem is to determine the most economical dimensions of a rectangular tank capable of holding 1,000 cubic feet.

It is self evident that if the bottom of the copper tank is ten feet square, 10 multiplied by 10 gives 100 as the area of the bottom, which multiplied by 10 for the depth, gives the correct dimensions of a tank which will hold 1,000 cubic feet.

A cube ten feet square will hold 1,000 cubic feet it is true, but that would require 500 feet of copper (100 on the bottom and each of the four sides). The point of our problem is to determine the most economical form of a tank that will hold 1,000 cubic feet and use the least possible amount of copper.

It is a simple every-day piece of shop work which any mechanic would tackle in a way satisfactory to himself, but which mathematicians will discover involves the "duplication of the cube."

19 The Hidden Star

CAN YOU find a perfect five-pointed star in the above pattern?

20 ***Divide a Greek cross into the fewest number of pieces which will fit together to form two Greek crosses of identical size.***

IN THE whole realm of puzzledom there is nothing so fascinating as the series of problems pertaining to the form of the Greek cross and its peculiar relations to the square, parallelogram, and other symmetrical shapes.

Instead of the well-known problem of converting the cross into a square by the fewest number of cuts, attention is called to the following pretty feat of changing one cross into two.

It appears that one of our wounded boys in blue, returning home after being nursed back to life by a faithful Red Cross lassie, begged the red cross from her arm as a keepsake. She, in true sweetheart style, took her scissors and by a few deft clips, cut the cross into several pieces which could be fitted together perfectly to make two crosses of the same size. It is a simple but beautiful trick, and the satisfaction of guessing it will be as great as if you should win a prize.

21 *Slide the numbered blocks into serial order.*

OLDER INHABITANTS of Puzzleland will remember how in the seventies I drove the entire world crazy over a little box of movable blocks which became known as the "14-15 Puzzle." The fifteen blocks were arranged in the square box in regular order, but with the 14 and 15 reversed as shown in the above illustration. The puzzle consisted of moving the blocks about, one at a time, to bring them back to the present position in every respect except that the error in the 14 and 15 was corrected.

A prize of $1,000, offered for the first correct solution to the problem, has never been claimed, although there are thousands of persons who say they performed the required feat.

People became infatuated with the puzzle and ludicrous tales are told of shopkeepers who neglected to open their stores; of a distinguished clergyman who stood under a street lamp all through a wintry night trying to recall the way he had performed the feat. The mysterious feature of the puzzle is that none seem to be able to remember the sequence of moves whereby they feel sure they succeeded in solving the puzzle. Pilots are said to have wrecked their ships, and engineers rush their trains past stations. A famous Baltimore editor tells how he went for his noon lunch and was discovered by his frantic staff long past midnight pushing little pieces of pie around on a plate! Farmers are known to have deserted their plows, and I have taken one such instance as an illustration for the sketch.

Several new problems which developed from the original puzzle are worth giving:

Second Problem — Start again with the blocks as shown in the large illustration and move them so as to get the numbers in regular order, but with the vacant square at upper left-hand corner instead of lower right-hand corner (see Fig. 1).

Third Problem — Start with the blocks as before, turn the box a quarter-way round and move the blocks until they rest as in Fig. 2.

Fourth Problem — Start as before, then shift the pieces until they form a "magic square," the numbers adding to thirty along all vertical and horizontal rows, and the two diagonals.

1	2	3	
4	5	6	7
8	9	10	11
12	13	14	15

Fig. 1

Fig. 2

22 *The Ailing Nephew*

HERE IS an odd little problem in relationships that has an amusing answer. Uncle Reuben was in the big city to visit his sister, Mary Ann. They were walking together along a city street when they came to small hotel.

"Before we go any farther," Reuben said to his sister, "I should like to stop a moment and inquire about a sick nephew of mine who lives in this hotel."

"Well," replied Mary Ann, "seeing as I don't happen to have any sick nephew to worry about, I will just trot on home. We can continue our sightseeing this afternoon."

What relation was Mary Ann to that mysterious nephew?

THE MAN WITH
    THE HOE
BY SAM LOYD

23 *Show how the two farmers divided their earnings.*

THE FOLLOWING simple puzzle is really so devoid of mathematical difficulties that I hesitate to introduce it. Yet, like the celebrated poem by Edwin Markham, I believe that it opens the door to an interesting discussion.

It appears that for five dollars Hobbs and Nobbs agreed to plant a field of potatoes for Farmer Snobbs. Nobbs can drop a row of potatoes in forty minutes and cover them at the same rate of speed. Hobbs, on the other hand, can drop a row in only twenty minutes, but while he is covering two rows, Nobbs can cover three.

Assuming that both men work steadily until the entire field is planted, each man doing his own dropping and covering, and further, assuming that the field consists of twelve rows as shown, how should the five dollars be divided so that each man is paid in proportion to the work accomplished?

THE GOLD BRICK PUZZLE

24 *What happens to the missing square inch?*

THIS PUZZLE shows how easily a person can be deceived when he is buying a gold brick. The large square in the illustration represents the gold brick which the farmer has just purchased from the top-hatted stranger. Its sides are divided evenly into 24 parts.

If the square is 24 inches on the side, then it must contain 24 times 24, or 576 square inches. Note the diagonal line from corner to corner. We cut the square on this line, then move the top piece up one space along the incline. If we snip off the small triangular piece A, which will be projecting from the right side, we can replace it in the triangular space at B in the upper left corner.

We have now formed a rectangle that is 23 inches wide and 25 inches high. But 23 times 25 is only 575 square inches! What happened to that missing square inch?

It is said that the last volume written by Euclid was devoted entirely to geometrical fallacies such as this; problems and puzzles which contained cleverly concealed errors. Unfortunately the work was lost, but surely it must have been one of the grandest books ever attempted by the author.

25 How deep is the lake?

THE POET Longfellow was a fine mathematician who often spoke about the advantages of clothing mathematical problems in such attractive garb that they would appeal to the fancy of the student instead of following the dry, technical language of the textbooks.

The water lily problem is one of several introduced in Longfellow's novel, *Kavanagh*. It is so simple that anyone, even without a knowledge of mathematics or geometry, could solve it, yet it illustrates an important geometrical truth in a never-to-be-forgotten way. I forget the exact language of the problem, as Longfellow described it to me personally during a discussion on the subject, but it concerns a water lily growing in a lake: The flower was one span above the surface of the water, and when swayed by the breeze would touch the surface at a distance of two cubits, from which data one could compute the depth of the lake.

Now, let us suppose, as shown in the sketch, that the water lily is ten inches above the surface of the water, and that if it were pulled over to one side it would disappear under the surface at a point twenty-one inches from where it originally stood. What is the depth of the water?

26 *How many steps are in the old tower?*

TOURISTS WHO have taken a summer outing along the Jersey coast are familiar with the old Beacon Tower at Point Lookout. The ruins of the tower, which once served as a lighthouse for more than half a century, stand in the last stages of dissolution upon a little ledge of rocks that runs out into the sea. The accompanying picture is taken from a sketch made some fifty years ago, obtained from an old resident now in his ninety-sixth year. He recalls the erection of the tower when he was a very small boy. The entire county turned out to honor the event and there were few persons in that neighborhood who did not believe that the old Beacon was just a little bit higher than the tower of Babel.

There is nothing left now but a charred post some sixty feet high, the stairs having been destroyed by fire twenty odd years ago. But the picture as well as the county records show that it was originally 300 feet high.

This was then a very respectable height indeed. For over a century the limit of one's powers of conception of height around the city of New York was to say, "As high as Trinity Church steeple." But times have changed since that era and it was only the other day that Trinity's venerable sexton complained that boys in the adjoining office building were throwing things down on the church spire.

The center support of the Beacon Tower was composed of huge poles skillfully spiked together, about which there wound a spiral staircase with an iron hand rail. This rail went exactly four times around the column, as shown in the sketch. There was one baluster or picket to each step, and as these pickets were just one foot apart, it should really be a simple matter to determine how many steps one had to take to reach the top. Yet to quote the words of Captain Huff, who furnished the picture and history of the tower, "I never yet knew one of them city folks who come out here for the summer who could figure it out right."

To summarize the data: the tower was 300 feet high from the ground to the top of the last step, the hand rail circled the tower four times, and the pickets in the rail, one to each step, were a foot apart. To this we must add that the diameter of the entire tower (that is, the diameter of the imaginary cylinder around which the rail twines) was twenty-three feet, ten and one-half inches. How many steps were on the circular staircase?

27 *Trading Chickens*

A FARMER and his good wife are at the market to trade their poultry for livestock on the basis of eighty-five chickens for a horse and a cow. It is understood that five horses are exactly equal in value to twelve cows.

"John," the wife said, "let us take as many more horses as we already have selected. We will then have only seventeen horses and cows to feed through the winter."

"I think we should have more cows than that," replied her husband. "Moreover, I find that if we double the number of cows we have picked, it would give us nineteen horses and cows in all, and we would have just enough chickens to trade for them."

These unsophisticated country people knew nothing about algebra, yet they knew to a feather just how many chickens they had and the number of horses and cows they were to get. Our puzzlists are asked to determine, from the data given here, how many chickens the farmer and his wife took with them to the market.

28 *Tell how many different routes there are and which is shortest.*

HERE IS an odd puzzle, interesting not only on account of the general principle involved, but because of its antiquity and the curious history connected with it. Königsberg, the second capital of Prussia, is divided by the River Pregel into four quarters, including the island of Kneiphof, as shown on the accompanying map. There are eight bridges connecting the different parts of the town, and there is a puzzle connected with them which greatly vexed the good citizens of Konigsberg over two hundred years ago.

A promenade, embracing a tour of the bridges, had always been an amusement and recreation for the young people. According to old accounts, somehow or other the question was raised as to how long it would take to make a tour of the bridges. This led to the startling assertion that a complete tour of all bridges — without going over any bridge more than once — was impossible.

It is a matter of history that a committee of young folks visited Leonard Euler, the mathematician, in 1735 and asked him to decide the point at issue. A year later Euler presented a voluminous report to the Academy of Sciences of St. Petersburg, wherein he claims to have demonstrated the impossibility of solving the problem. This appears in the report of the Academy, 1741, vol. 8, and has been published in French and English by noted mathematicians, since it treats of the principle as applied to any number of bridges. Professor W. Rouse Ball, of Trinity College, discusses the antiquity and merits of the problem in his great work, *Mathematical Recreations*, but errs in ascribing its origin to Euler in 1736, and makes the remarkable statement that there were and still are, according to Baedeker, but seven bridges. The oldest records refer to eight, and our map presents an accurate tracing from Baedeker, who especially refers to the eight bridges. Euler was a very young man in 1735, and was not a famous mathematician until nearly fifty years later, so he may have fallen into the error of starting from some locations which, like certain combinations of my 14-15 puzzle, will not work out.

The question of returning to the starting point does not enter into the problem at all. It is merely a matter of proving it possible to start from a certain spot in town and go to another spot by passing over all bridges but once. The reader is asked to tell how many different ways this can be done, and which way is shortest.

29 *The Chess Playing Colonel*

During my visit to St. Petersburg I met Tschigorinsky, the Russian chess expert, who told me that at the outbreak of the Russo-Japanese unpleasantness he was put in command of an army station where 20 regiments were continually in process of formation, 100 men per week being added to each regiment. On the last day of every week the regiment having the most men would be sent to the front.

It so happened at a time when the first regiment had 1,000 men, the second 950, the third 900, and so on down, decreasing 50 each step to the twentieth, which had but 50, that Gen. Tschigorinsky, found that the colonel of the fifth (which had 800 men) was a capital chess player. So, in order to keep him from being advanced to the front, which would occur in five weeks, he allotted him but 30 men every week instead of 100 as given to the others.

Assuming that 20 regiments are being continually recruited, can you tell just how many weeks it was before our chess-playing colonel had to go to the seat of war?

Uncle Sam's Fob Chain

BY Sam Loyd

30 How many different watch fob chains can be made with the five pieces?

I WAS shown a curious fob chain the other day, patterned after the old custom of carrying a string of coins attached to a watch. This particular chain consisted of four coins and the figure of an eagle. The coins, as shown, were punched respectively with five, four, three, and two holes, so that the small links which joined them together might have been placed differently, to furnish quite a variety of patterns.

This feature of being able to produce a series of fob chains, each consisting of a string of four coins connecting the watch to the pendant eagle, gave rise to quite a discussion regarding the number of possible arrangements which can be made from the five pieces without any two being exactly similar. What is your opinion?

The Four Elopements
BY SAM LOYD

31 Ferry four jealous couples across the river.

OF COURSE all good puzzlists are familiar with the time-honored problem of the man who had to ferry a fox, a goose, and some corn across a river in a boat which would carry but two at a time. The story of the four elopements, equally old, is built upon similar lines, but presents so many complications that the best or shortest answer seems to have been overlooked by mathematicians who have considered the subject.

It is told that four men eloped with their sweethearts, but in carrying out their plan were compelled to cross a stream in a boat which would hold but two persons at a time. In the middle of the stream, as shown in the sketch. There is a small island. It appears that the young men were so extremely jealous that not one of them would permit his prospective bride to remain at any time in the company of any other man or men unless he was also present.

Nor was any man to get into a boat alone when there happened to be a girl alone, on the island or shore, other than the one to whom he was engaged. This leads one to suspect that the girls were also jealous and feared that their fellows would run off with the wrong girl if they got a chance. Well, be that as it may, the problem is to guess the quickest way to get the whole party across the river.

Let us suppose the river to be two hundred yards wide, with an island in the middle on which any number can stand. How many trips would the boat make to get the four couples safely across in accordance with the imposed conditions?

32 *The Eccentric Teacher*

HERE IS a remarkable age problem which I am sure will amuse the young folks and at the same time open up a new line of reasoning for some of the wiseacres who make a specialty of statistical calculations.

It appears that an ingenious or eccentric teacher, as the case may be, desirous of bringing together a number of older pupils into a class he was forming, offered to give a prize each day to the side of boys or girls whose combined ages would prove to be the greatest.

Well, on the first day there was only one boy and one girl in attendance, and, as the boy's age was just twice that of the girl's, the first day's prize went to the boy.

The next day the girl brought her sister to school. It was found that their combined ages were just twice that of the boy, so the two girls divided the prize.

When school opened the next day, however, the boy had recruited one of his brothers. It was found that the combined ages of the two boys were exactly twice as much as the ages of the two girls, so the boys carried off the honors that day and divided the prize between them.

The battle waxed warm now between the Jones and Brown families, and on the fourth day the two girls appeared accompanied by their elder sister; so it was then the combined ages of the three girls against the two boys. The girls won of course, once more bringing their ages up to just twice that of the boys. The struggle went on until the class was filled up, but our problem does not need to go further than this point. Tell me the age of that first boy, provided that the last young lady joined the class on her twenty-first birthday.

It is a simple but pretty puzzle, calling for ingenuity rather than mathematics and yielding readily to puzzle methods.

MILITARY TACTICS BY SAM LOYD

33 *Show how a military division could enter gate number 1, march across all sixty-four squares, and leave by the other gate after passing under the triumphal arch.*

MANY REMEMBER the sensation created by General Winfield Scott's remarkable saying to Secretary of War Stanton, "While we have scores of commanders who could march a division of soldiers into a park, not one of them knows enough about military tactics to get them out again!" The remark was accepted as a scathing criticism of what were termed our holiday parade soldiers.

I knew General Scott as a skillful chess player, and now recall the fact of building a curious chess puzzle which I intended to present to him, if occasion occurred, to illustrate the military tactics of a division of soldiers passing through a public park.

It does not require a knowledge of chess, as it is a puzzle, pure and simple; but to facilitate explanation, I have taken the liberty of marking the park off into squares which resemble a checkerboard. The problem, however, is quite pretty. Show

how a military division should enter at gate No. 1, march through all of the squares, under the triumphal arch, and out through gate No. 2, making the fewest possible number of turns. All moves must be like a chess rook's, and no square can be visited more than once.

Mark an 8 x 8 diagram of 64 squares upon a piece of paper and then essay with a pencil to pass over every square, beginning and ending at the gates shown, and passing under the arch. It is safe to say you will make several attempts before you get the shortest possible answer, which is so pretty that you will know when you have guessed it.

THE STOUT BOY QUARTETTE COULD TUG JUST AS STRONG AS THE PLUMP SISTERS

WHILE TWO PLUMP SISTERS AND A STOUT BOY COULD HOLD THEIR OWN AGAINST THE SLIM TWINS

SLIM TWINS AND THREE PLUMP SISTERS vs. ONE PLUMP SISTER AND FOUR FAT BOYS

34 Which side will win the last event?

THE FOOT·BALL·PROBLEM BY· SAM LOYD

35 *How large is the football?*

I AM not protected with a patent cast-iron nose, so I shall not jeopardize that organ by sticking it into a game with which I am not familiar. Armored ribs and padded shins were not in vogue in my student days. We used to play football with our feet, as the name implies, and never tried to kill or maim the opposing players.

My puzzle, however, will have nothing to do with "rushes," "punts," "touchdowns," or even high kicking. It is simply a little reminiscence of the days when we country boys loved to kick the old-fashioned soft rubber ball about the green.

We lived way back in the country and used to order our ball by mail, according to sizes, as advertised in a sporting house catalogue which advised patrons to "give the exact number of inches required." That is where the problem comes in.

We were told to give the required size in inches, but we did not know whether it meant the number of inches of rubber on the surface or the number of cubic inches of wind contained in the ball, so we combined the two principles and ordered a ball which would contain just as many cubic inches of air as it had superficial inches of surface!

How many of our puzzlists can guess the diameter of the ball that was ordered?

36 *How many acres are in the interior triangular lake?*

I WENT to Lakewood the other day to attend an auction sale of some land, but did not make any purchases on account of a peculiar problem which developed. The land was advertised as shown in the posters on the fence as 560 acres, including a triangular lake. The three plots show the 560 acres without the lake, but since the lake was included in the sale, I, as well as other would-be purchasers, wished to know whether the lake area was really deducted from the land.

The auctioneer guaranteed 560 acres "more or less". This was not satisfactory to the purchasers, so we left him arguing with some katydids, and shouting to the bullfrogs in the lake, which in reality was a swamp.

The question I ask our puzzlists is to determine how many acres there would be in that triangular lake, surrounded as shown by square plots of 370, 116 and 74 acres. The problem is of peculiar interest to those of a mathematical turn, in that it gives a positive and definite answer to a proposition which, according to usual methods, produces one of those ever-decreasing, but never-ending decimal fractions.

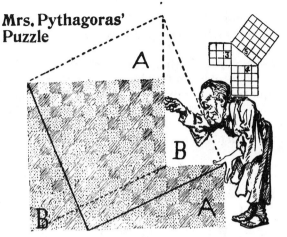

Mrs. Pythagoras' Puzzle

37 *Without destroying the checked pattern, cut the shape into three pieces that will form a checkered square.*

WHEN MRS. PYTHAGORAS took counsel with her spouse regarding the best way of squaring the checked remnant of Athenian matting shown above, the great philosopher gave the following explanation of how this could be done.

The dotted line on the matting is clearly the hypotenuse of a right triangle whose sides are the sides of two squares that together form the remnant. According to Pythagoras' great theorem, this line must be the side of a square possessing an area equal to the combined area of the two squares on its sides. (The theorem is illustrated in the small figure at the upper right corner.) Once we have obtained this length, we can then cut the remnant as shown by the two solid lines and refit the three pieces to form a square. This method can be used to make a perfect square from any two square pieces.

"Now, Thag," said Mrs. Pythagoras, for she always called him that in the house, "I am feared these goods will fray if they are cut on the bias, so I want to get along without that hippopotamus line. Here is a plan which will also do it in three pieces: Cut out that long piece marked A, and stand it on end at one side; then move piece C down one step, and it forms a 13 x 13 square, all right, all right."

"But, I don't like it altogether, Thag," she continued, "you see the pattern don't run quite right on the squares in that long piece. Can't you find a perfect answer without giving any of the squares that half turn?"

There we have Mrs. Pythagoras' new puzzle.

[To make the problem a bit clearer, note that the threads on the black squares all run diagonally NE by SW. When piece A is turned to the vertical position, the threads run NW by SE. Mrs. P. wants a three-piece solution that will preserve both the checked pattern and a uniform direction for all the threads. — MG]

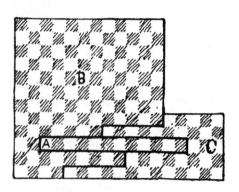

38 *The Three Brides*

OLD MONEYBAGS let it be known that he would endow his daughters with their weight in gold, so they were speedily suited with suitable suitors. All were married on the same day, and before weighing in partook of some exceedingly heavy wedding cake, which made the grooms very light-hearted.

Collectively, the brides weighed three hundred and ninety-six pounds, but Nellie weighed ten pounds more than Kitty, and Minnie weighed ten pounds more than Nellie. One of the bridegrooms, John Brown, weighed just as much as his bride, while William Jones weighed half again as much as his bride, and Charles Robinson twice as much as his bride. The brides and grooms together weighed half a ton. The puzzle is to tell the full names of the three brides after they were married.

A PROBLEM IN
DIAMONDS and RUBIES.
By Sam Loyd

39 Guess the size of two stones which are exchanged for a pair of earrings.

IT IS worth knowing that diamonds increase in value according to the squares of their weights, while rubies increase according to the cubes of their weights. For example, if a fine diamond of one karat is worth $100, a two-karat stone of the same quality would be worth $400, a three-karat gem of equal purity would be worth $900. If a fine Oriental ruby of one karat is worth $200, a two-karat stone would be worth $1,600.

A noted merchant, familiar with the diamond mines of Brazil, Cape Colony, and other quarters of the globe, showed me a pair of diamond earrings which he had exchanged for two diamonds of different sizes on the basis of a single karat being worth $100, as explained. Can you guess the size of the two stones of different sizes which he exchanged for a pair of earrings of uniform size? Of course there are many answers, so you are asked to find the smallest possible sizes of the two stones which equal the value of two of different sizes, without employing fractions of a karat.

THE ✦JOINER'S✦ PROBLEM ∼BY∼ SAM LOYD.

40 *Cut the board into the smallest number of pieces which will form a perfect square.*

STUDENTS OF geometry will find here an interesting elementary problem which can best be solved by experimental puzzle methods, although there is a scientific rule for getting the correct answer which bears a close resemblance to the famous forty-seventh proposition of Euclid. The joiner has a piece of board four feet long by two feet wide, with a corner clipped off. The puzzle is to divide the board into the fewest number of pieces, so that without any waste they will fit together and make a perfect square top for the table shown in the picture.

In this particular case the missing piece has been cut off at an angle of fifteen degrees, but when you solve the puzzle you will find that the cutting procedure will work just as well when this angle is greater or less than shown here.

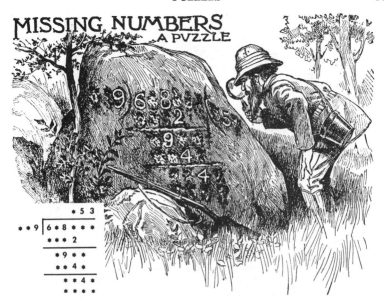

MISSING NUMBERS
A PVZZLE

```
         * 5 3
* * 9 | 6 * 8 * * *
        * * * 2
        -------
        * 9 * *
        * * 4 *
        -------
        * * * 4 *
        * * * *
```

41 Can you restore the missing digits?

THE ARCHEOLOGIST is examining a completed problem in long division, engraved on a sandstone boulder. Due to weathering of the rock, most of the figures are no longer legible. Fortunately, the eight legible digits provide enough information to enable you to supply the missing figures.

It really looks as if there should be scores of correct answers, yet so far as I am aware, only one satisfactory restoration of the problem has been suggested.

42 The Mathematical Cop

"THE TOP o' the mornin' to you, officer," said Mr. McGuire. "Can you tell me what time it is?"

"I can do that same," replied Officer Clancy, who was known on the force as the mathematical cop. "Just add one quarter of the time from midnight until now to half the time from now until midnight, and it will give you the correct time."

Can you figure out the exact time when this puzzling conversation occurred?

43 *At exactly what time will the two hands next be together?*

EVERYONE HAS heard of the famous race between Achilles and the tortoise. Achilles could walk twelve times faster than the tortoise, so Zeno, the Greek philosopher, arranged for a race in which the tortoise would have a twelve-mile head start. Zeno maintained that Achilles would never overtake the tortoise because while he walked twelve miles, the tortoise would advance one mile. Then when Achilles went the one mile, the tortoise would have gone one-twelfth of a mile. There would always be a small distance between them, although this distance would grow smaller and smaller.

We all know of course that Achilles does catch up with the tortoise, but it is not always easy in circumstances of this sort to determine the exact point of passing. In the picture Tommy has just realized the similarity between the famous Greek race and the movements of the hands on the clock. It is now exactly noon so the two hands are together. Tommy is wondering exactly when the hands will next be together again. (By "exactly" we mean the time must be expressed accurately to the fraction of a second.)

It is a most interesting problem, forming the groundwork on which numerous clock puzzles of a fascinating character have been built. For this reason a clear understanding of the principles involved is recommended to all earnest puzzlists.

44 School of Sea Serpents

THE CROP of sea serpents has been unusually large this year, and many new varieties have been seen at the seaside resorts. The yarns of the Nantucket skippers are as thrilling as ever, and for such a time-honored theme are remarkably original.

The advent of the kodak, however, has disillusioned the public mind and placed the sea serpent industry upon a substantial business basis. Exaggerated yarns of the old salts and professionally authenticated log books are no longer accepted unless backed up by a set of photographs.

One sea captain claimed that while he was becalmed off Coney Island he was surrounded by a school of sea serpents, many of which were blind.

"Three could not look from their starboard blinkers," he reported, "and three could not look to larboard. Three could look to starboard, three to larboard; three could look both to starboard and larboard, while three had both their optics out of commission." So it was duly entered on the logbook and duly sworn to that "there were eighteen serpents in sight."

But a couple of camera fiends who got a focus on the school of monsters have developed their negatives in a way that negatives the whole story and reduces the number of serpents to the minimum of possibilities. Just how many serpents belonged to that school?

The Pony Puzzle

45 *Rearrange the six pieces to make the best possible picture of a horse.*

MANY YEARS ago, when I was returning from Europe in company with Andrew G. Curtin, the famous war Governor of Pennsylvania (returning from his post in Russia to seek nomination for president of the United States) we discussed the curious White Horse monument on Uppington Hill, Berkshire, England.

If you know nothing about that weird relic of the early Saxons, the accompanying sketch will afford an excellent idea of its appearance. It represents the figure of a colossal white horse, several hundred feet long, engraved on the side of the mountain about a thousand feet above the level of the sea and easily seen for a distance of some fifteen miles. It is more than a thousand years old, and is supposed to have been carved there by the soldiers of Ethelred and Alfred (a white horse was the emblem of the Saxons) after their victory over the Danes. What looks like a patch of snow on the side of the mountain is in reality produced by the green turf being removed to show the white chalk beneath in the form of a horse.

After the white horse had been thoroughly discussed, the governor banteringly exclaimed, "Now, Loyd, there would be a capital subject for a puzzle."

Many a good puzzle idea has come from just such a tip. So, with my scissors and a piece of silhouette paper, I speedily improvised the accompanying figure of a horse.

It would be a simple matter to improve the parts and general form of the old horse, and I did modify it in the version which I afterward published, but somehow I love the old nag best as first devised, with all its faults, so I now present it as it actually occurred to me.

The world has been moving rapidly during the last decade, and puzzlers are much sharper than they used to be. In those days very few, probably not one out of a thousand, actually mastered the puzzle, so it will be a capital test of the acumen of the past compared with that of the present generation to see how many clever wits of today can solve it.

Trace an exact copy of the figure as shown. Cut out the six pieces very carefully, then try to arrange them to make the best possible figure of a horse. That is all there is to it, but the entire world laughed for a year over the many grotesque representations of a horse that can be made with those six pieces.

I sold over one thousand million copies of "The Pony Puzzle." This prompts me to say that whereas I have brought out many puzzles, patented numerous inventions, and devoted much time and money, to my sorrow, upon the "big things," more money is made from little things like "The Pony Puzzle," which do not require a five-dollar bill to promote and place on the market.

GOING INTO ACTION

A NAVAL PUZZLE BY SAM LOYD

46 *Show how the big battleship can run down the sixty-three enemy vessels and return to the starting point in the fewest possible number of straight dashes.*

THE ACCOMPANYING sketch shows a signalman running up the flags of battle, which for the benefit of all who are not familiar with naval signals, will be explained to represent the once famous battle cry during the American-Spanish war, "Remember the Maine!" The commander is shown mapping out the plan of attack by which he intends to ram and run down the flotilla of enemy gunboats, so as to destroy them with the greatest possible dispatch.

Commencing at the point occupied by the large battleship, mark out with one continuous line the sixty-three little boats and return to the starting point, making the fewest possible "straight" moves, as we term it in puzzle language.

47 *How much should the lady pay to have her necklace made?*

I WILL take occasion to remark that because some of my puzzles are well known does not imply that every one is familiar with the answers to them. The correct answers to some of the most popular ones have never been published, and, so far as I am aware, have never really been guessed. I will illustrate this point by presenting the "Necklace Puzzle," which I showed several years ago, and which every one who sees it flatters himself that he solves it at once. Yet I do not remember any one who really found the correct answer.

It is based on an everyday business transaction, intended to show how the average mortal goes the wrong way about doing anything which calls for the slightest mathematical knowledge or ability. It is devoid of all semblance of catch or subterfuge, and there is no "missing link" mystery about it. It was given to all of the leading jewelers and chain makers of New York, who said they would have no use for a salesman or employee who could not see through such a simple transaction, yet not one of them gave the correct answer.

A lady bought twelve pieces of chain, as shown in the border of the picture, and wished to have them made into an endless necklace of 100 links. The jeweler said it would cost 15 cents each to cut and join a small link and 20 cents to cut and join a large link. The question is to tell how much the lady should pay to have the necklace made. That is all there is to it, and it is a pretty problem for the young folks.

48 *Cow, Goat, and Goose*

A DUTCHMAN with a goat and a goose met a milkmaid leading a cow, whereupon the maiden screamed with terror.

"What frightens you?" asked Hans.

"You are going to kiss me against my will," said the coy maid.

"How can I do that with these cranky animals on my hands?" asked Hans.

"What prevents you from thrusting your cane into the ground so as to fasten the goat to it and then put your goose under my pail?" queried the maiden.

"Because that cross-looking cow might hook me," said Hans.

"Oh, that fool cow wouldn't hook nobody, and what is to prevent you from driving all three of them into my pasture field?" replied the terrified maiden.

And right here comes a most interesting puzzle, for during the subsequent discussion the following facts developed. They found that the goat and goose together would eat just as much grass as the cow, so if that field would pasture the cow and goat for forty-five days, or the cow and goose sixty days, or the goat and goose for ninety days, how long would it pasture the cow, the goat, and the goose? Early replies are requested, as Hans and Katrina are contemplating a speedy partnership.

THE BATTLE OF THE FOUR OAKS

PROBLEM BY SAM LOYD

49 *Divide the field into four identical parts, each containing a tree.*

THE TOWN of Four Oaks derives its name from the fact that one of the early settlers, who owned a large tract of land, left it to four sons with the stipulation that they "divide it into equal portions, as indicated by the positions of four ancient oaks which had always served as landmarks."

The sons were unable to divide the land amicably, since the four trees really furnished no clue to guide them, so they went to law over it and squandered the entire estate in what was known as the "battle of the four oaks." The person who told me this story thought it might form the groundwork for a good puzzle, which it has done, so far as suggesting a theme is concerned.

The picture represents a square field with four ancient oak trees, equal distance apart, in a row from the center to one side of the field. The property was left to four sons who were instructed to divide the field into four pieces, each of the same shape and size, and so that each piece of land would contain one of the trees. The puzzle is an impromptu one, gotten up on the spur of the moment, so it is really not very difficult. Nevertheless it is safe to say that everyone will not hit upon the best possible answer.

50   *How much does the baby weigh?*

MRS. O'TOOLE, being of an economical turn of mind, is trying to weigh herself, her baby, and her dog for one cent. If she weighs a hundred pounds more than the combined weights of dog and baby, and if the dog weighs sixty per cent less than the baby, can you determine how much the little cherub weighs?

51 *Rearrange the eight pieces to form a perfect checkerboard.*

IN THE history of France is told an amusing story of how the Dauphin saved himself from an impending checkmate, while playing chess with the Duke of Burgundy, by smashing the chess board into eight pieces over the Duke's head. It is a story often quoted by chess writers to prove that it is not always politic to play to win, and has given rise to a strong line of attack in the game known as the King's gambit.

The smashing of the chess board into eight pieces was the feature which always struck my youthful fancy because it might possibly contain the elements of an important problem. The restriction to eight pieces does not give scope for great difficulty or variety, but not feeling at liberty to depart from historical accuracy, I shall give our puzzlists a simple little problem suitable for summer weather. Show how to put the eight pieces together to form a perfect 8 x 8 checkerboard.

The puzzle is a simple one, given to teach a valuable rule which should be followed in the construction of puzzles of this kind. By giving no two pieces the same shape, other ways of doing the puzzle are prevented, and the feat is much more difficult of accomplishment.

52 *How does the moonshiner measure $21.06 worth of "Mountain Dew?*

Of course we have all heard the problem about the man with the barrel of honey who met a customer with a three and a five-quart pitcher, who wanted to purchase four quarts of honey. It is a simple matter to juggle the honey around with the two measures until we get the required four quarts, but just exercise the gray matter of your brain and see if you can discover in how few changes the feat can be performed.

That well known feat will prepare your mind for our present juggling puzzle, which is to guess how that moonshiner, with a barrel of applejack and a barrel of cider (31½ gallons to a barrel) can give his customer $21.06 worth of "Mountain Dew" as they term mixed applejack and cider. The moonshiner has only the two and four-gallon measures to juggle with, and the customer wants a full twenty-six gallons in his keg.

First determine what proportions of cider and applejack in twenty-six gallons of Mountain Dew will cost exactly $21.06, then see if you can discover the fewest number of manipulations the moonshiner has to make to fill the keg with the required amounts.

Multiplication and Addition

By SAM LOYD

$$2 \times 2 = 4 \qquad a \times b = y$$
$$2 + 2 = 4 \qquad a + b = y$$

53 *Give different values for* $A \times B = y$ *and* $A + B = y.$

THE TEACHER in the sketch is explaining to his class the remarkable fact that 2 times 2 gives the same answer as 2 plus 2.

Although 2 is the only number with this property, there are many pairs of different numbers which can be substituted for A and B in the equations on the right of the blackboard. Can you find such a pair? They may be fractions of course, but they must have a product which is exactly equal to their sum.

54 *Select a twelve-letter word and change its position in the fewest number of moves.*

HERE IS an interesting word puzzle built along the lines of my old 14-15 puzzle. There is supposed to be a letter placed upon each of the twelve movable blocks, which reading from top downward spell a correct word. The puzzle is to slide the blocks into the horizontal groove so as to make the word read correctly from left to right.

It will be readily understood that any twelve-letter word may be employed to solve the puzzle, but that every word will produce different results. Some words are better than others, and it is largely a matter of luck and experiment to find the word which will solve the puzzle in the fewest possible number of manipulations.

55 *Which player should pay for the game?*

THREE MEN began a game of fifteen-ball pool and, according to the custom of the pool hall, agreed that the loser would have to pay for the game. Player No. 1, who was an expert, agreed to pocket as many balls as players No. 2 and No. 3 together. Just as they were going to start, a fourth man came in and joined them. Since he was a stranger, he did not receive any handicap odds, playing on even terms with each of the other three players.

The rack shows the number of balls which each man made during the play. A discussion then ensued as to who was the loser.

The puzzle is to tell which player should pay for the game according to the terms of agreement. That the problem is not so simple as it looks may be inferred from the fact of its having been referred to the competitors in a recent championship pool tournament where it was found that no two players agreed on the same answer. Which man should pay for the game and why?

56 *How can you score exactly fifty points?*

A FRIEND and I were taking in the side shows at Coney Island the other day when we came to what the man told us was the squarest game on the beach. There were ten little dummies which you were to knock over with baseballs. The man said: "Take as many throws as you like at a cent apiece and stand as close as you please. Add up the numbers on all the men that you knock down and when the sum amounts to exactly 50, neither more nor less, you get a genuine 25¢ Maggie Cline cigar with a gold band around it."

Our money gave out before we learned how to win, and we noticed that lots of people didn't smoke any more Maggie Clines than we did. Can you show how we might have made exactly 50 points?

THE ST. PATRICK'S DAY PARADE —BY SAM LOYD

57 *How many men were in the parade?*

DURING A recent St. Patrick's Day parade an interesting and curious puzzle developed. The Grand Marshall issued the usual notice setting forth that "the members of the Honorable and Ancient Order of Hibernians will parade in the afternoon if it rains in the morning, but will parade in the morning if it rains in the afternoon. This gave rise to the popular impression that rain is to be counted as a sure thing on St. Patrick's Day. Casey boasted that he "had marched for a quarter of a century in every St. Patrick's day parade since he had become a boy."

I will pass over the curious interpretations which may be made of the above remark, and say that old age and pneumonia having overtaken Casey at last, he had marched on with the immortal procession. When the boys met again to do honor to themselves and St. Patrick on the 17th of March, they found that there was a vacancy in their ranks which it was difficult to fill. In fact, it was such an embarrassing vacancy that it broke up the parade and converted it into a panic-stricken funeral procession.

The lads, according to custom, arranged themselves ten abreast, and did march a block or two in that order with but nine men in the last row where Casey used to walk on account of an impediment in his left foot. The music of the Hibernian band was so completely drowned out by spectators shouting to ask what had become of "the little fellow with the limp," that it was deemed best to reorganize on the basis of nine men to each row, as eleven would not do.

But again Casey was missed, and the procession halted when it was discovered that the last row came out with but eight men. There was a hurried attempt to form with eight men in each row; again with seven, and then with five, four, three, and even two, but it was found that each and every formation always came out with a vacant space for Casey in the last line. Then, although it strikes us as a silly superstition, it became whispered through the lines that every time they started off, Casey's "dot and carry one" step could be heard. The boys were so firmly convinced that Casey's ghost was marching that no one was bold enough to bring up the rear.

The Grand Marshal, however, was a quick-witted fellow who speedily laid out that ghost by ordering the men to march in single file; so, if Casey did follow in spirit, he brought up the rear of the longest procession that ever did honor to his patron saint.

Assuming that the number of men in the parade did not exceed 7,000, can you determine just how many men marched in the procession?

58 *The Three Napkins*

"BETSY ROSS wasn't so much of a much with her star cutting stunt, I don't think," said the office boy. "That trick is so dead easy it gives me a pain. She wouldn't be one, two, three in it with the girls over at the restaurant. Oh my! but ain't they the cut-ups for fair!

"Here's a puzzle Maggie showed me the other day, that's a puzzle as is a puzzle: Take three napkins, each a foot square, then tell me how big a square table could you cover with those three napkins?

"There ain't no cutting. Just lay them down, lapped or folded, and see how big a square the three will cover."

PUZZLE OF THE Red Spade BY SAM LOYD

59 *Show how to change the spade into a heart by cutting it into three parts.*

DURING A recent visit to the Crescent City Whist and Chess Club my attention was called to the curious feature of a red spade which appears in one of the windows of the main reception room. The design came from Dresden, and, after the manner of cathedral windows, is made of numerous small pieces of stained glass skillfully fitted together to make the desired pattern.

No reason was ever vouchsafed, nor even asked for, regarding the incongruousness of the color. It was looked upon as a blunder which occasioned considerable comment at first, but came to be looked upon afterwards with favor, not only on account of the novelty of such a thing as a red spade, but also because a black spade would have made the room too dark.

Hearing, however, that a blunder had actually been committed by the manufacturer, in that the ace of hearts was to have been the insignia of the club, I was led to examine the window carefully. The spade was composed of three pieces and

I speedily discovered that by rearranging the pieces they would fit together to form the ace of hearts, as originally desired. The members have become so accustomed, not to say endeared, to their unique emblem that they would not consent to having it changed. Nevertheless it makes a unique although simple puzzle.

60 *The Missing Pennies*

HERE IS a puzzle known as the Covent Garden Problem, which appeared in London half a century ago accompanied by the somewhat surprising assertion that it had mystified the best mathematicians of England. The problem is continually cropping up in some form or other, generally accompanied by that same statement of its having baffled the European mathematicians, all of which must be taken with a liberal allowance of salt. Our Yankee scholars should find so little difficulty in dispelling the mystery that I can only feel justified in presenting it as a special practice problem for our juvenile puzzlists.

It is told that two huckster ladies were selling apples at the market when Mrs. Smith, for some reason or other which must be the real mystery that baffled the mathematicians, was called away. She asked Mrs. Jones, the other apple lady, to dispose of her stock for her.

Now, it appears that they each had an equal number of apples, but Mrs. Jones had larger fruit and was selling hers at the rate of two for a penny, while Mrs. Smith sold three of hers for a penny. Upon accepting the responsibility of disposing her friend's stock, Mrs. Jones, wishing to be very impartial, mixed them all together and sold them off at the rate of five apples for two pence.

When Mrs. Smith returned the next day the apples had all been disposed of, but when they came to divide the proceeds they found that they were just seven pence short. It is this shortage which has disturbed the mathematical equilibrium for such a long period.

Supposing that they divided the money equally, each taking one-half, the problem is to tell just how much money Mrs. Jones lost by the unfortunate partnership.

61 *What are the odds against the giraffe?*

JUST TO show how little many people who are infatuated with the races really know about the theory of chances, we ask the following simple question:

If the odds are two to one against the hippopotamus and three to two against the rhinoceros, what should be the odds against the giraffe if everything is on the square, as it always is in Puzzleland?

Here is a second puzzle connected with the same picture:

If the giraffe can beat the rhinoceros one-eighth of a mile in a two mile race, and the rhinoceros can beat the hippopotamus one-quarter of a mile in a two mile race, by what distance could the giraffe beat the hippo in a two mile race?

62 *Stamps for a Dollar*

A LADY gave the postage stamp clerk a one dollar bill and said, "Give me some two-cent stamps, ten times as many one-cent stamps, and the balance in fives." How can the clerk fulfil this puzzling request?

FREE ACRES   A squatter problem
BY
SAM LOYD

63 *How can you enclose as many acres of land as there are twelve-foot rails to a fence?*

HERE IS a pretty puzzle from the Lone Star State, introducing a famous old problem and a bit of American history
with which many of our readers are doubtless familiar. Texas
was practically settled, or rather overrun, by the Americans
as far back as 1830, but it was not until the end of fifteen years
of fighting with the Mexicans and Indians that it was admitted
into the Union. Shortly after that date the famous squatter
law was introduced which gave a settler free all the land he
could inclose or cultivate within a year from the time of taking
possession.

Some of the early settlers had pretty hard times, but the
descendants of such as managed to "stick it out," as they
termed it, now rank among the great cattle kings of the world,
and, according to an official report just issued, some of the
most wealthy landed proprietors of the world are Indians.
Among the great ranches of the West, whose owners would
not be appalled by the size of the flocks of "white bulls and
dappled bulls that grazed on the plains of Sicily," as grandilo-
quently described by Archimedes, may be mentioned the comfortable ranch of Texas Pete, a half-breed Indian. He was

among the first to take up land under the squatter act which gave him ownership of all the land he could inclose or cultivate within one year. According to his own story — and he is still a hale and hearty man, although well beyond the three score years and ten allotment — he and his wife were to receive all the land they could inclose with a three-rail fence within twelve months, so for one whole year he and his wife were putting up this fence. From this story we derive the following curious problem: Let us suppose that the tract of land is exactly square and is inclosed by a three-rail fence, as shown in the sketch, and that each rail is exactly twelve feet long. If we assume that there are just as many acres inclosed as there are rails in the entire fence (and recall that 43,560 square feet make one acre), then how many acres of land are in Texas Pete's great cattle ranch?

64 *Lord Rosslyn's System*

THE RECENT statement that some one had won 777,777 francs at Monte Carlo recalls the principle of Lord Rosslyn's system, promulgated a few yars ago.

Without going into the technicalities of the play of roulette as practiced at Monte Carlo, we will accept the statement that Lord Rosslyn's system was based upon the principle of playing the multiples of seven, and ask our puzzlists to tackle the following simple problem.

Suppose that a player (merely betting on red or black, where the chances are even), lays down a single franc piece seven times in succession and then whether he won or lost raises the stakes to 7 francs and again plays seven times. He then bets 49 francs seven times; then 343 francs seven times; then 2,401 fancs seven times; then 16,807 francs seven times; then 117,649 francs seven times. If by thus playing 49 times he chanced to win 777,777 francs, how many times did he win to gain that amount?

This is somewhat simple, nevertheless interesting at the present time as illustrating the utter absurdity of what became known for some time as "Rosslyn's lucky system."

If you cannot produce the exact sum of 777,777 francs at first, a few experimental trials will show that the puzzle is not so mathematical as it looks.

THE GREAT COLUMBUS PROBLEM.

PRIZE PUZZLE
BY
Sam Loyd

65 How can the first player always win?

I RECENTLY came across a vividly written description of the fifteenth-century craze for gambling, wherein, among other games of skill or chance upon which the cavaliers were wont to bet so recklessly, mention was made of the sport of laying eggs upon a cloth. Here possibly was the true origin of the Columbus egg story, which despite its clever moral has always seemed too tame for such a fierce period. I saw that there was a pretty principle involved that calls for ingenious and original lines of thought.

It is simply a game to be played between two opponents who place eggs of uniform size alternately upon a square napkin. After an egg is placed it must not be moved or touched by another one. This continues until the napkin is so crowded that it is not possible to place another egg. The last person who placed an egg is the winner, and since the size of the napkin or the eggs, as well as the variable distances which may occur between them, are of no importance, it would seem as if the question of placing the last egg was a matter of luck or chance. Yet the first player can always win by a clever strategy which, as the great navigator remarked, "is the easiest thing in the world when you are shown how!"

66 How large will their flocks become?

THE IMPLICIT faith which the ancient Greeks, Romans, and Egyptians placed in the oracles of their gods can best be appreciated when we realize that from the declaration of a war down to the trading of a cow, no transaction of any kind whatever was undertaken without the advice and approbation of oracles. In the famous painting of Jupiter at Dodona, two peasants are shown to be consulting the oracle about some trifling affair, and are directed in a commanding way toward a mirror.

To illustrate the overwhelming importance and dignity, or rather of mystery with which things of insignificance were surrounded, the puzzle sketch shows two poor peasants who wish to know whether the great Jupiter will smile auspiciously upon the purchase of a little lamb and goat.

"They shall increase," said the oracle, "until the sheep multiplied by the goats gives a product which, reflected in the sacred mirror, will show the number of the entire flock!"

There is a certain ambiguity and mystery about the words of the oracle, nevertheless we present it for the consideration of our puzzlists.

THE YACHT RACE
— BY SAM LOYD —

67 *How long did it take the yacht to win?*

IN THE sketch above, the two yachts are on the first leg of a race on a triangular course from buoy A to B to C, then back to A again.

Three landlubbers on the winning yacht tried to keep a record of the boat's speed, but all three became violently seasick and their records suffered accordingly. Smith observed that the yacht sailed the first three-quarters of the race in three and a half hours. Jones noted only that it did the final three-quarters in four and a half hours. Brown was so anxious to get back on land that the best he could do was observe that the middle leg of the race (from buoy B to C) took ten minutes longer than the first leg.

Assuming that the buoys mark an equilateral triangle and that the boat had a constant speed on each leg, can you tell how long it took the yacht to finish the race?

THE BATTLE OF HASTINGS
A PUZZLE OF SQUARES
BY SAM LOYD

68 How many men were in Harold's army?

ALL STUDENTS of history know of the mystery and uncertainty concerning the details of the ever-memorable battle which occurred on the fateful October 14, 1066. This puzzle deals with a curious passage from this battle's history which has not received the attention it deserves.

The passage in question, as pointed out by Professor Henry Dudeney, says: "The men of Harold stood well together, as their wont was, and formed thirteen squares, with a like number of men in every square thereof, and woe to the hardy Norman who ventured to enter their redoubts, for a single blow of a Saxon war-hatchet would break his lance and cut through his coat of mail. * * * When Harold threw himself into the fray the Saxons were one mighty square of men, shouting the battle cries of 'Ut!' 'Olicrosse!' 'Godemite!' "

Contemporary authorities agree that the Saxons did actually fight in that solid formation. In the "Carmen de Bello Hastingensi," a poem attributed to Guy, Bishop of Amiens, it tells how "the Saxons stood fixed in a dense mass." And Henry of Huntingdon speaks of "the square like unto a castle, impenetrable to the Normans."

If Harold's forces were divided into thirteen squares, which, when he added himself to the number, could be arranged into one large square, then how many men must there have been? The puzzle is so difficult that few mathematicians are likely to solve it correctly.

69 The Canals on Mars

HERE IS a map of the newly discovered cities and waterways on our nearest neighbor planet, Mars. Start at the city marked T, at the south pole, and see if you can spell a complete English sentence by making a tour of all the cities, visiting each city only once, and returning to the starting point.

When this puzzle originally appeared in a magazine, more than fifty thousand readers reported, "There is no possible way." Yet it is a very simple puzzle.

MIXED TEAS
BY
SAM LOYD

70 *What are the proportions of green tea to black?*

IN THE Orient the blending of teas is such an exact science that combinations of different kinds of teas are figured to the millionth part of an ounce! It is said that formulas which belong to some noted growers of tea have been kept secret for hundreds of years and cannot be imitated.

Just to illustrate the complications that arise in the science of blending teas and to show the difficulty of penetrating the mystery with which the art is surrounded, attention is called to a simple puzzle based upon two blends only.

The mixer has received two cases, each cubical but of different sizes. The larger cube contains black tea, the smaller cube contains green tea. He has mixed together the contents and found that the mixture exactly fills twenty-two cubical chests of equal size. Assuming that the interior dimensions of all the chests can be expressed to the exact decimal, can you determine the proportion of green tea to black? [In other words, find two different integers such that when their cubes are added, the result can be evenly divided by twenty-two to obtain a number that has an integral cube root.—M.G.]

PLATO'S CUBES
A classical problem,

BY

71 *How many cubes are in the monument and square?*

REFERENCE IS often made to the classical legend of the Delian problem of duplicating or doubling the area of a cube. Philoponus tells how the Athenians, in 432 B.C., suffering from the plague, consulted Plato in regard to it. They had previously conferred with the oracle at Delos, and Apollo had told them that they must double the size of the golden altar of the temple. This they were unable to do. Plato, the greatest mathematician as well as philosopher of his day, told them that they were being punished for their willful neglect of the sublime science of geometry, and deplored that they had not one man among them sufficiently wise to solve the problem.

The Delian Problem, which is neither more nor less than the duplication of the cube, is so generally confounded with that of Plato's Cubes that writers who are not up in mathematical lore get them sadly mixed. The latter is sometimes referred to as Plato's Geometrical Numbers, and is usually accompanied by the statement that little or nothing is known about the true conditions of the problem. Some writers maintain that its terms are lost.

There is an ancient description of a massive cube erected in the center of a tiled plaza, and it requires no stretch of imagination to associate this monument with Plato's problem. The sketch shows Plato gazing upon the huge marble cube which is constructed out of a given number of smaller cubes. The monument rests in the center of a square plaza, paved with similar small cubic blocks of marble. There are just as many cubes in the pavement as there are in the monument, and they are precisely of the same size. Tell how many cubes are required to construct the monument and the square plaza upon which it stands, and you will have solved the great problem of Plato's Geometrical Numbers.

72 *The Deadwood Express*

THE DEADWOOD Express arrived at a western mining town with a consignment of two boxes for a young lady. A lively dispute quickly developed between the expressman and the lady's miner friends.

The difficulty was that the expressman wished to charge for the boxes at the rate of $5 per cubic foot, as per his instructions on the freight bill. The miners, however, strenuously objected on the grounds that their custom was invariably to pay so much per running foot — according to mining laws. They could not see what right an express company had to meddle with the "cubic contents" of a young lady's box, anyway!

The expressman was compelled to accept the proposed terms, so he measured the length of the boxes and charged $5 per running foot. Both boxes were perfectly cubical and one was exactly half the height of the other.

The strange part of the problem is that when the expressman placed the two boxes together and measured their combined length it was found that there was not the thousandth part of a cent difference in the ways of charging — at $5 per cubical foot or at $5 per running foot.

What were the sizes of the two boxes?

It is a simple yet interesting puzzle, which will cause the gray matter in the brains of our mathematicians to circulate somewhat before hitting upon the proper answer.

After Dinner Tricks
BY SAM LOYD

73 *Pick up two adjacent glasses at a time and in four moves change the positions so that each alternate glass will be empty.*

FOR READERS interested in parlor tricks, here is an amusing puzzle which can be used advantageously to amuse the guests after a banquet or at an evening party. In the former case eight wine glasses — four empty and four partially filled — illustrate the trick to perfection.

In this, as in all exhibitions of a similar character, everything depends upon the skill and clever acting of the performer. He must have his little book down to perfection, so as to be able to do the trick forwards or backwards without the slightest hesitation, while by the aid of a ceaseless flow of conversation he impresses upon his hearers the fact of its being the most simple little trick that ever happened, which anyone can do unless he be a natural born muttonhead or hopelessly befuddled. It really looks so simple that almost anyone will be lured into accepting an invitation to step up and test his sobriety by showing how readily he can perform the feat and then the fun begins — for it will rattle ninety-nine out of a hundred.

The problem is stated below the sketch. The glasses in the picture are numbered to make it easy to describe the correct procedure.

74 Find a numbered route from the center to the outside of the woods.

EULER, THE great mathematician, discovered a rule for solving all manner of maze puzzles, which, as all good puzzlists know, depends chiefly upon working backwards. The puzzle above, however, was built purposely to defeat Euler's rule, and out of many attempts is probably the only one that thwarts his method.

Start from that heart in the center. Go three steps in a straight line in any one of the eight directions, north, south, east, west, or on the bias, as the ladies say, northeast, northwest, southeast, or southwest. When you have gone three steps in a straight line you will reach a square with a number on it, which indicates the second day's journey, as many steps as it tells, in a straight line in any one of the eight directions. From this new point, march on again according to the number indicated, and continue on in this manner until you come upon a square with a number which will carry you just one step beyond the border. You will then be out of the woods and can holler all you want, for you will have solved the puzzle!

75 *The Quarrelsome Couples*

AS A PREFACE to a very interesting problem which shows how a party of quarrelsome picnickers might cross a stream in the same boat without upsetting it, I shall take for granted that all puzzlists, young and old, are familiar with the clever tactics of the boatman who had to ferry a fox, a goose, and some corn across a river in a small boat just "built for two."

In this version a party of three married couples returning from a picnic were compelled to cross a stream in a small boat. The boat would hold but two at a time, and none of the ladies could row.

It so happened that Parson Cinch, a popular preacher, had quarreled with the other two gentlemen of the party. As a result, Mrs. Cinch had a falling out with the other ladies.

How is it possible for the gentlemen to conduct them all across the stream in such a way that no two disagreeing parties shall ever cross over together or even remain on either side of the stream at the same time. Another curious feature of the strained relations in this story is that no one gentleman should remain on either side with two ladies.

The puzzle is merely to show how many times the little two-seated boat must cross the stream in order to ferry the entire party over; but I take occasion to say that not one person out of a thousand is endowed with a headpiece which could figure it out mentally, without recourse to pencil and paper, although the faculty of doing so may readily be acquired.

76 *Into how few squares, containing one or more pieces of patchwork, can the quilt be divided?*

THE SKETCH represents the members of the "Willing Workers" society overwhelming their good parson with a token of love and esteem in the shape of a beautiful patchwork quilt. Every member contributed one perfectly square piece of patchwork consisting of one or more small squares.

Any lady would have resigned if her particular piece of work was tampered with or omitted, so it became a matter of considerable study to find out how to unite all the squares, of various sizes, together to form one large square quilt. Incidentally it may be mentioned that since every member contributed one square piece of patch quilt, you will know just how many members there were when you discover into how few square pieces the quilt can be divided. It is a simple puzzle which will give considerable scope for ingenuity and patience.

77 *What two strokes can run the course in the lowest score?*

EVERYBODY IS playing golf now, and even the lazy ones who a few weeks ago declared how much pleasanter it was to swing in a shady hammock, have caught the golf fever and are chasing the ball around the golf links. I am not much of a golfer, but I have met a genius who has a winning system based on mathematics. He says: "Just cultivate two strokes of different lengths, one a drive, the other an approach, and play directly toward the hole so that a combination of the two distances will get you there."

What should be the proper lengths of strokes to learn that would make possible the lowest score on a nine-hole course, of 150 yards, 300 yards, 250 yards, 325 yards, 275 yards, 350 yards, 225 yards, 400 yards, and 425 yards? The ball must go the full length on each stroke, but you may go beyond the hole with either stroke, then play back toward the hole. All strokes are on a straight line toward the hole.

THE DANISH FLAG
PUZZLE
—BY—
SAM LOYD

78 *Give the dimensions of a cross which will be as large in area as the rest of the flag.*

ANENT THE recent fruitless negotiations by Uncle Sam for the purchase of the Danish West Indies, several unique legends were brought to light regarding the titles of that group of the Virgin Islands.

St. John, St. Thomas and St. Croix, which constitute the Danish West Indies, were among the first discoveries of Columbus in 1492. For centuries they were considered of no value whatever, so when some shipwrecked Danes raised their flag as a signal of distress, the title passed into their hands without dispute, and according to custom was named after the patron saints of the mariners.

The Danish flag is so seldom seen that comparatively few persons know that it is a white cross upon a red field, and I have never known the ensign to be constructed according to the regulations, which stipulate that half of the field should be white. Supposing, for instance, that the proportions of the flag are five feet wide by seven and a half feet long, how many of our puzzlists can find a simple rule which gives the width of a white cross that will take up exactly one-half the space?

79 *Cut the mosaic into parts which will form two squares.*

IT IS not generally known that the celebrated piece of Venetian mosaic by Domenichino, known as the Guido collection of Roman heads, was originally divided into two square groups, discovered at different periods. They were brought together and restored to what is supposed to be their correct form, in 1671. Apparently by accident it was discovered that each of the two squares consisted of pieces which would fit together into one 5 x 5 piece as shown.

It is a pretty puzzle, and as many puzzles, like mathematical propositions, can be worked backward to advantage at times, we will reverse the problem and ask you to divide the large square into the fewest number of pieces which can be refitted into two squares.

This puzzle differs from the Pythagorean principle of cutting lines on the bias. We know that two squares can be divided by diagonal lines to produce one larger square, and vice versa, but in this puzzle we must cut on the lines only, so as not to destroy the heads. It may also be mentioned, incidentally, that students who have mastered the Pythagorean problem will not find much difficulty in discovering how many heads there must be in the smaller squares.

Problems of this kind, which call for the "best" answer in the "fewest number of pieces," offer great scope for cleverness. In this problem the best solution does not destroy any heads or turn any of them upside down.

80 *False Weights*

THE MONEY of the East, coined in variable sizes and weights to facilitate the swindling of travelers, is too complex for our mathematicians to handle, so in describing the following manner of trading among the Orientals we will simplify matters by talking in dollars and cents.

Camels' hair, which enters largely into the manufacture of shawls and expensive rugs, is gathered by what is known as the common people and sold through a commission broker, in small or large lots, to the merchants. To insure impartiality, the broker never buys for himself, but upon receiving an order to buy, finds some one who wishes to sell, and charges 2 percent commission to each of them, thereby making 4 percent on the transaction. Nevertheless, by juggling with the scales, he always manages to add to this profit by cheating, the more especially if a customer is green enough to place any confidence in his word or pious exclamations.

I take occasion to call attention to a pretty puzzle connected with a transaction which aptly illustrates the simplicity of his methods. Upon receiving a consignment of camel's hair he placed the same upon the short arm of his scales, so as to make the goods weigh one ounce light to the pound, but when he came to sell it he reversed the scales so as to give one ounce to the pound short, and thus made $25 by cheating.

It appears to be — and as a matter of fact is — a very simple problem, with clear and sufficient data for the purpose. Nevertheless, it will tax the cleverness of an expert bookkeeper to figure out a correct answer to the question of how much the broker paid for the goods.

GRANDFATHER'S PROBLEM
— BY —
SAM LOYD

81 *What is the difference in weight between six dozen dozen pounds of feathers and half a dozen dozen pounds of gold?*

HERE IS one of those old-time problems that are passed down through the generations without anyone having the temerity to question the accepted answers. Recently, however, a juvenile puzzlist in Boston had this antique gem sprung on him by his grandfather. He responded with such an unexpected solution that it really took the wind out of his grandparent.

Most people have been asked so often to state the difference in weight between six dozen dozen pounds of feathers and half a dozen dozen pounds of gold that they answer without a

moment's hesitation. "A pound's a pound the world over,"
they say. "Six dozen dozen would be 864 and half a dozen
dozen would be 72, making a difference of 792 pounds."

Yet if the question is asked again in all seriousness, and you
give sufficient thought to the matter, you will discover that it
has never really been answered correctly since it was first pro-
pounded in 1614.

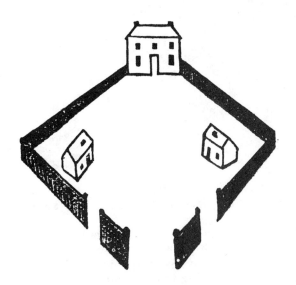

82 *The Quarrelsome Neighbors*

THIS ODD little puzzle was one of my earliest productions,
published more than half a century ago. Reproduced above is
the original drawing which I made when a lad of nine.

It is told that three neighbors who shared a small park, as
shown in the sketch, had a falling out. The owner of the large
house, complaining that his neighbor's chickens annoyed him,
built an enclosed pathway from his door to the gate at the
bottom of the picture. Then the man on the right built a path
to the gate on the left, and the man on the left built a path
to the gate on the right

None of the paths crossed. Can you draw the three paths
correctly?

A·PUZZLING·MIXTURE

BY SAM LOYD

83 *With how much water did the milkman dilute each of his two cans of milk?*

IT IS told that an honest and unsophisticated milkman, who had boasted much about his conscientious dealings and the fact of his never having disappointed a customer, found to his dismay one morning that his supply of milk was inadequate to the demands of his patrons. In fact, his stock was much too short to serve his route, and there was no possibility of getting any more milk.

Realizing the serious effect this might have on his business, to say nothing about the disappointment and inconvenience to his customers, he was at his wits' end to know what to do.

After turning the matter carefully over in his mind he decided that he was too conscientious and fair-minded to show partiality by serving some and passing others. He would have to divide what he had among them all, but would dilute his milk with a sufficient quantity of water to make it meet all demands.

Having found, after diligent search, a well of exceedingly pure water which he could conscientiously employ for the purpose, he pumped into one of the cans as many gallons of water as would enable him to serve all of his customers. Having been in the habit, however, of selling two qualities of milk, one for eight cents a quart and the other for ten, he proceeded to produce two mixtures, in the following ingenious manner.

From Can No. 1, which contained only water, he poured enough to double the contents of Can No. 2, containing the milk. Then from No. 2 he poured back into No. 1 just as much of the mixture as he had left water in No. 1. Then, to secure the desired proportions, he proceeded to pour back from No. 1 again just a sufficient quantity to double the contents of No. 2. This left an equal number of gallons in each can, as may be readily shown, although there were two gallons more of water than milk in can No. 2.

Now, this is not as complicated as it looks, for it requires but three changes to equalize the contents of the two cans. Can you determine exactly how much milk and water each can finally contained?

84 *The Stenographer's Salary*

HERE IS a problem from the ordinary affairs of life which is as interesting as it is puzzling to all who tackle it. The "Boss" was feeling pretty good the other day, so he said to his stenographer:

"Now, Mary, in view of the fact that you never indulge in useless vacations, I have determined to raise your salary $100 every year. Beginning from today, for the ensuing year you will be paid weekly at the rate of $600 a year; next year at the rate of $700, the next at $800, and so on, always increasing $100 per year."

"On account of my weak heart," replied the grateful young woman, "I suggest that it would be safer to make the change less abrupt. Start the salary from today on the basis of $600 a year, as suggested, but at the end of six months raise the yearly salary $25, and continue to give me a $25 yearly raise every six months, so long as my services are satisfactory."

The boss smiled benignly upon his faithful employee as he accepted the amendment, but a twinkle in his eye set some of the boys to figuring whether or not the boss made a wise move by accepting her proposition. Can you tell?

TELL MOTHER'S AGE
PROBLEM
BY
SAM LOYD

85   How old is the mother?

AGE PUZZLES are always interesting, and possess a certain fascination for young folks who are at all mathematically inclined. As a rule, they are extremely simple, but in this problem the data is so meager, and the proposition so different from what is expected, that the query actually appears startling.

One of the trio in the picture was having a birthday anniversary. This aroused Master Tommy's curiosity regarding their respective ages, and in response to his queries his father said:

"Now, Tommy, our three ages combined amount to just seventy years. As I am just six times as old as you are now, it may be said that when I am but twice as old as you, our three combined ages will be twice what they are at present. Now let me see if you can tell me how old is mother?"

Tommy, being bright at figures, readily solved the problem, but then he had the advantage of knowing his own age and could guess pretty closely the ages of the others. Our puzzlists, however, have merely the data regarding the comparative ages of father and son, followed by the startling question, "How old is mother?"

86 *Show how to score 96 with three "doublets."*

As a veteran marksman who has participated in many matches, I was greatly interested in the recent pistol match by cable, wherein the Americans proved their superiority over the Frenchmen, although it was a pretty close score — 4889 to 4821. The shooting took place simultaneously on both sides of the ocean, and the results were cabled back and forth, which made the match an exciting and interesting one.

I was amused by the comments of uninitiated spectators who were greatly mystified by the language of the marksmen. They seemed to be continually calling out hours of the day strangely at variance with the correct time. Many persons gravely explained that it referred to the difference in time between New York and Paris.

"What time did you shoot?" one expert would ask another. "Half-past five, but I think I will try half-past four."

To explain this I must point out that it is necessary on longer ranges to make allowance for wind and distance. All marksmen, therefore, look upon their targets as representing the dial of a clock, so if, when firing straight at the bull's eye the ball hits down where the figure five would be, a marksman must now fire at eleven o'clock to score a "plumb center."

Some problems developed during the match which I am certain would interest our puzzlists. Here, for instance, is one which struck me as being so pretty that I am sure it will repay you for the trouble of solving it.

One of the marksmen scored 96 with six shots, but it required a close examination of his target to learn that he had scored three "doublets," as they term the feat of passing two bullets through the same hole.

The target which the two umpires are examining shows how the rings are marked for scoring. Can you find a way of making three doublets that will give a total score of 96 points?

87 The Strange Building Loan Plan

AN OCCASIONAL problem of unique character, drawn from the affairs of ordinary life, is often instructive. Here is one built upon a common, every-day transaction which everyone can understand whether he knows anything about mathematics or not. As a matter of fact, it was suggested and carried out by a man so deficient in common arithmetic that he could not compute simple interest, and had such a fear of being cheated at figures that he would not make the deal in any other way than that explained below.

It seems that he wished to buy a piece of property, but having only a small amount to pay down and having an abhorrence of figures, mortgages, and interest, said he would not make the purchase unless he could get it upon what he termed the "building loan plan." He would pay down $1,000 and make five more payments of $1,000 each at the end of every twelve months. Such payments were to cover the entire cost of the property, including the interest up to the date of each of the five payments.

The sale was made according to the terms stated, but as the money was actually worth just 5 per cent a year to the party who sold, the question is to determine how much he really got for the property.

88 *Explain how to climb the ladder in the fewest number of steps.*

THE BOY in the sketch has just proposed the following unusual problem to the hod carrier:

Start on the ground, then move alternately up and down the ladder, one rung at a time, until you finally end on the top rung. You must go up and down in such fashion that you are on the ground once again, that you step only twice on the top rung, and that all other rungs are stepped on an equal number of times.

For example, you might climb all the way to the top, then all the way to the ground, then back up to the top again. In this way you would meet all the conditions in twenty-seven steps. Your problem is to meet the conditions in the fewest possible number of steps. It's safe to say you may have to go up and down that ladder many times before you hit on the correct answer!

89 How did the burglars divide the full and empty bottles equitably?

HERE IS a little study in subtraction and division which shows the importance of elementary arithmetic. Solvers with an aversion to figures, however, need not be deterred from tackling the puzzle, for the subtraction and division here referred to calls for the cleverness of a Sherlock Holmes rather than the learning of a mathematician.

It appears that a gentleman's wine cellar had been burglarized to the extent of two dozen bottles of wine which the robbers carried off and might have kept if they had been as proficient in division as they were in subtraction.

They stole a dozen quarts and a dozen pints of champagne, but finding the same somewhat heavy to carry, they proceeded to reduce the weight by drinking off five quarts and five pints to the success of their respective candidates in the next aldermanic election. To leave no traces behind, as well as on account of their value, they took the empty bottles with them. On reaching their rendezvous, however, they could not hit upon an equitable division of seven full quarts and five empty ones, and seven full pints and five empty pints, so that each should have the same value in bottles and wine. Perhaps the division would not have been so difficult if they had not already imbibed so freely as to muddle their brains.

Not knowing enough to keep "mum," which was very essential in this case, they quarreled and made a great racket. This attracted the attention of a couple of policemen who descended upon them and drank all the champagne which had cost them so much labor to secure. But that, as well as what became of the empty bottles, like the question as to how their heads felt in the morning, has nothing to do with this puzzle.

Without asking me for any further information, as I do not wish to appear to know too much about this transaction, I ask you to tell me how many burglars there were and how they might have divided their seven quarts of wine and seven pints of wine, and the five empty quart bottles and the five empty pint bottles so that each man would have an equitable share. Of course it is assumed that no wine is to be transferred from one bottle to another. Any reputable burglar knows that champagne can not be handled in that manner, so there is no opportunity of introducing a clever juggling trick in connection with the puzzle.

90 Count The Votes

HERE IS a simple but pretty problem which developed at a recent election where 5,219 votes were cast for four candidates. The victor exceeded his opponents by 22, 30, and 73 votes, yet not one of them knew how to figure the exact number of votes received by each.

Can you give a simple rule for obtaining the desired information?

THE BOXER'S PUZZLE

91 *What is the best play and how many boxes will it win?*

HERE IS a familiar little puzzle game from the East, played upon lines very similar to the well known game of "Tit-Tat-Toe, three in a row." One of the Chinese girls writes sixteen letters on a slate in four rows, as shown. After marking a straight dash from A to B, she passes the slate to her opponent, who connects E with A. If the first player should now connect E with F, the other player would connect B with F and score "one box," and have the right to play again. But they have played so well that neither one has yet scored a box, although each has played six times. The game is reaching a critical point where one of them must win, for there are no draws in this game.

The little maiden sitting down has to play now, and if she connects M to N her opponent could score four boxes in one run, then having the right to one more play, would connect H and L which would win all the rest. What play would you now advise, and how many boxes will it win against the best possible play of the second player? Remember, when a player scores a "box" he plays again. Suppose for example a player marks from D to H. Then the second player marks from H to L, and no matter what mark the first player makes, the second player scores all nine boxes without stopping. It is a game that calls for considerable skill as you will discover after trying a few games.

92 The Dutchmen's Wives

SOME OF the old Dutch customs are still preserved in this country, such as trading cattle, poultry, and farm products in odd numbers and quantities, buying eggs by the score, some things by the dozen, others by bushel, peck, or small measure, sugar by the three and half pounds, and so on.

A curious old problem, published a couple of centuries ago in a unique collection of anecdotes about old Manhattan, illustrates the involved way in which the Dutch settlers made their purchases. In the language of this quaint volume: "There came three Dutchmen of my acquaintance to see me, who, being recently married, brought their wives with them. The men's names were Hendrick, Claas, and Cornelius; the women's Geertring, Catrun, and Anna, but I forgot the name of each man's wife. Well, they told me that they had been to market buying hogs, each person buying as many hogs as they gave shillings for one hog. Hendrick bought 23 hogs more than Catrun, and Claas bought 11 more than Geertring. Likewise they said that each man laid out three guineas (or 63 shillings) more than his wife. Now, what I want to know is whether it is possible from this description of their purchases to tell the name of each man's wife?"

The inference was that the merry party got so befuddled over their beer and schnapps that they could not tell just who was who, so the worthy landlord was compelled to sort out the different couples properly by a process of extracting square roots.

It is a curious problem which yields readily to experimental puzzle methods.

93 Cut the mitre-shaped piece of paper into the fewest number of pieces which will form a perfect square.

ANY ONE who has ever presented a puzzle or trick to a party of friends is acquainted with Alec and his habit of showing, or attempting to show, that he knows all about the trick before it has been explained. In case he happens to have seen the puzzle, he gives away the answer before those who take interest in such matters have a chance to try it. Even when it is new to him, he aims to show how it resembles something else which he can readily demonstrate to be superior to this one. Generally his explanation reminds us of the Persian proverb, "He who knows not, and knows not that he knows not, is a nuisance." It is a pleasure to squelch him, as in the following instance:

Harry is about to show his young friends a clever cutting puzzle when he is rudely interrupted by Alec the Terrible, who believes it to be what is familiarly known among puzzlists as the famous old Mitre puzzle. This is a puzzle that I sprang upon the public over fifty years ago, calling for a method of cutting the paper into four pieces of identical shape and size.

In response to Alec's boisterous offer to explain the puzzle to every one, Harry promptly replies:

"All right! The puzzle is to cut this paper into the fewest possible number of pieces which will fit together to form a perfect square. I have forgotten the answer myself, but my friend here has kindly volunteered to explain it."

The puzzle is not as easy as it looks, and is liable to baffle an expert a long time before he hits on the correct answer. Of course there are innumerable ways of doing the feat by cutting the paper into many pieces, but considerable ingenuity is required to do the job in the smallest number.

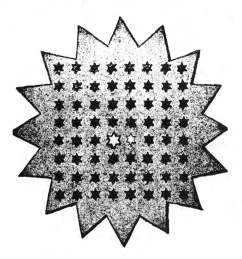

94 Heclai's Path

THIS PUZZLE is designed to show the erratic path of the comet Heclai, which starts from the small white star, destroys the entire constellation of sixty-two dark stars, and ends by exploding the large white star. Start at the small white star, then draw the fewest number of connected straight lines that will pass through each black star and end on the big white one.

95 Find the simplest method by which the trains can pass.

IN THIS specimen of primitive railroading we have an engine and four cars meeting an engine with three cars. The problem is to ascertain the most expeditious way of passing the two trains by means of the side-track, which is only large enough to hold one engine or one car at a time.

No ropes, poles or flying switches are to be used, and it is understood that a car cannot be connected to the front of an engine. How many times is it necessary to back or reverse the directions of the engines to accomplish the feat, each reversal of an engine being counted as a move in the solution?

DUCK SHOOTING
AT BUZZARDS BAY
problem by Sam Loyd

96 *By changing the position of the fewest pos-sible number of the ten ducks, arrange them so there will be five rows of four in each row.*

THE SUBJECT of this puzzle is a familiar one to residents in the vicinity of Buzzard's Bay and introduces one of the many problems which have doubtless been noticed by all who revel in the pleasures of duck shooting.

There are a thousand and one problems connected with the sport, any one of which would be worthy of consideration, but with which our puzzlists are doubtless more familiar than myself, so I only refer to one little proposition which may be peculiarly characteristic of my style of duck shooting. Of course it is a great feat to get more than one duck at a single shot. As that can only be done by getting several of them in a line, it set me to studying the principle upon which Buzzard Bay ducks line up, and I may have hit upon something which my uniform lack of skill as a marksman enabled me to discover.

I noticed that the birds invariably approached in two rows, with a corporal bird, so to speak, on each side in charge of either line, so that, as shown in the sketch, one could figure out three lines of four-in-a-row. Now just as soon as I got a line on four of these birds I would blaze away in the hopes of getting several birds with one shot. I could readily have killed one bird or possibly two, but my ambition to get four or none led to my making the following interesting discovery. As soon as the smoke cleared away, so that I could open my eyes, I would find that the ten birds had reversed their direction, to reorganize somewhere back in the swamps. What I particularly noticed, however, was that while they came in the three four-in-a-row form as shown, they invariably scooted away in the shape of five rows, with four-in-a-row. Just how they made the change I never could see, on account of the smoke and confusion, but I noticed that the fewest possible number of birds had changed their positions, so it will afford me special pleasure to give credit to any lucky duck who will solve this little problem for me correctly.

The picture shows ten ducks advancing in three rows of four-in-line. Now reorganize them so there will be five rows of four-in-line, simply by changing the position of the fewest possible number of ducks. Incidentally, it will also show how many ducks Grover bags out of the flock.

The problem can be worked out practically by placing small counters upon the ducks in the picture and moving them around until you get five rows of four-in-a-row.

97 *Domestic Complications*

HERE IS a pretty little tangle from the ordinary affairs of life, which the good housewife solved in a minute, but which drove a mathematician to the verge of insanity.

Smith, Jones, and Brown, were great friends. After Brown's wife died, his niece kept house for him. Smith was also a widower, and lived with his daughter. When Jones got married, he and his wife suggested that they all live together. Each one of the party (male and female) was to contribute $25.00 on the first of the month for household expenses, and what remained at the end of the month was to be equally divided.

The first month's expenses were $92.00. When the remainder was distributed, each received an even number of dollars without fractions. How much money did each receive, and why?

The Crazy Clock of Zurich
BY SAM LOYD

98 When will the clock next show the correct time?

SWISS TOURISTS will recognize in the accompanying sketch a deserted church at a lonely spot near the outskirts of Zurich, and recall the weird story of its bewitched clock. Omitting the supernatural and mysterious features of the story, by which the tourist is regaled with many versions, it may be briefly stated that the church was built about the middle of the fifteenth century. It was furnished with a clock by the oldest citizen of the place, a man named Jorgensen, reputed to be the founder of the manufacture of clocks, for which the place has become noted.

The clock was started at six o'clock in the morning, accompanied by the display of ceremony with which any event of slightest importance is always inaugurated by the Swiss. Unfortunately, the hands of the clock had been mounted on the wrong pinions. The hour hand started off while the minute hand revolved twelve times slower, with what the peasants term the "dignity of the hour hand."

After the strange antics of the bewitched timepiece had been explained to the aged and infirm clockmaker, he insisted on being carired in his bed to witness the strange phenomenon. Due to an astonishing coincidence, when he arrived, the time as indicated by the clock was perfectly correct. This had such an effect on the old man that he actually died of joy. The clock, however, continued its strange antics and was looked upon as bewitched. No one was bold enough to repair or even wind it, so its works have rusted to pieces, and all that remains is the curious problem which I now propose.

If the clock was started at six o'clock, as shown in the picture, with the hour hand moving twelve times faster than the other as explained, when will the hands first reach a point which will indicate the correct time?

99 *How Old Will Smith Be?*

SMITH IS the actuary for a life insurance company, and so imbued with mortuary tables and columns of dates that he talks and dreams of little else. He hurries home to spring a statistical problem in the family circle, especially for the benefit of his wife, of whose mathematical powers he is prone to speak disparagingly. She caught him, however, a short time ago on a compact which will have the effect of muzzling him for some time to come, and may possibly cure him of talking shop at home.

After propounding one of his statistical conundrums, which did not meet with the enthusiastic reception which he thought it merited, he boastingly remarked that if his better half would give him any problem on dates or ages which he could not answer in ten minutes he would pledge himself not to propound another problem until the anniversary of that day. He probably meant for one whole year, but, as the proposition was made on the 29th day of February 1896, and leap years don't have yearly anniversaries, he was held to a literal interpretation of his promise.

The problem with which his wife gagged him was as follows: "Now, Tom, supposing that you were three times my age when first we met, and that I am now just the age you were then, and that when I am three times my present age our combined years will amount to exactly one hundred, can you tell just how old you will be on the next 29th day of February?"

100 *Into how few pieces need the table top be cut to complete the dog house?*

THE PICTURE tells its own story and does not require a Sherlock Holmes to tell us that the lads have found an old tool chest in the garret; that their mother is attending an afternoon meeting, and that it must be Thursday, when Bridget has her day out. There are other interesting features which suggest themselves, such as how Towser is to get out of the little door after the kids have nailed up the side of the dog house. That, however, is a problem for Towser to settle in his own way, so we will waste no time in getting to the real point of the puzzle.

What is the best way of cutting the square top of the kitchen table into the fewest number of pieces which will fit together so as to close up the open end of the dog house?

101 If the moon were made of green cheese, into how many pieces could you divide it with five straight cuts of a knife?

"SPEAKING ABOUT the possibility of treating disease through the influence of will power," says a noted specialist, in a recent contribution to a medical journal, "I wish to say that in Switzerland the power of imagination is so strong among the wild mountain swine herdsmen that they will eat their sour brown bread with great relish through believing that it is green cheese from the moon! They actually go through the motions of cutting the moon, and like little children quarrel over imaginary portions."

Not being interested in the Christian Science side of the question, I was merely struck by the possibility of an odd puzzle arising from the story. Therefore, indulging the foolish fancy of those men shown in the sketch, let us suppose that the expert carver of the party is speculating as to the greatest possible number of pieces into which he can divide the moon with five straight cuts of a knife. The wild herdsmen are unfortunately reduced to short rations in having the last quarter of the old moon to feast upon, so they are trying to make the most of it. Are you clever enough to help them?

With a pencil and ruler mark off the pictured moon with five straight lines and see how many pieces you can produce.

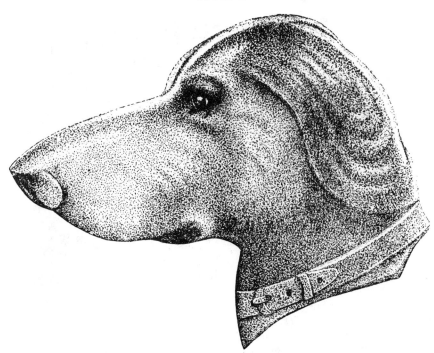

102 *How would you cut this gingerbread dog's head into two pieces of the same shape?*

HERE IS a practical problem in simple division calculated to baffle some of our puzzlists. You see, Toodles has received the present of a gingerbread dog's head and is told that she must divide it evenly with her little brother. In her anxiety to be fair and equitable in the matter, she wishes to discover some way to divide the cake into two pieces of equal shape and size.

How many of our clever puzzlists can come to her assistance by showing how the dog's head may be divided?

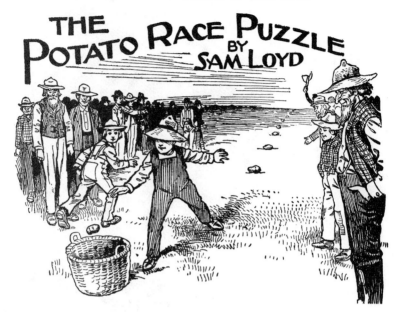

THE POTATO RACE PUZZLE
BY SAM LOYD

103 *Which boy will win?*

IN THE good old days no country fair was complete without a potato race, and in some localities the pastime is still popular with the rustic lads and lassies. A hundred potatoes are placed on the ground in a straight line, just ten feet apart. A basket is placed ten feet in back of the first potato. The two contestants start at the basket and race toward the first potato. Whoever gets it first carries it back to the basket while the other contestant goes after the second potato. In this manner the potatoes are carried one at a time to the basket, and the person who is the first to drop fifty potatoes in the basket is the winner.

Our first problem is to tell how far one person would travel if he started at the basket and gathered all one hundred potatoes one at a time.

Our second and much more difficult problem concerns a handicap race between Tom and Harry. Because Tom is 2.04 per cent faster than Harry, he is allowing Harry to select one potato and drop it in the basket before the race begins. In other words, to win the race Tom must gather fifty potatoes before Harry can gather his remaining forty-nine. The sketch shows Harry putting in the basket the one potato he has selected.

The result of the race will vary depending on which potato Harry selects. You are asked to determine which potato Harry should choose in order to increase his chances the most, and what the outcome of the race will be if he chooses correctly.

104

SAM LOYD'S
PUZZLING SCALES

SINCE THE SCALES NOW BALANCE

..AND BALANCE WHEN ARRANGED THIS WAY

THEN HOW MANY MARBLES WILL IT REQUIRE
TO BALANCE WITH THAT TOP?

105 *How would the year 1906 be written in the octamal system?*

To SHOW how difficult it is for the average person to leave the beaten track when thinking out some simple problem, let us take a look at the decimal system of numeration with which we are all familiar. It is safe to say that most people have given little thought to the subject. They see that any column can be built up to 9, but as soon as it gets above 9, it is carried over to the column on the left. They think it is so because it must be so, and can't help itself any more than 1 and 2 can help being 3. But this is far from the case. Primitive man originally learned to calculate upon the fingers of both hands, just as we see many people today utilizing their fingers in some every-day transaction. Hence the introduction of the decimal system. If the human race, as has been claimed, sprang from the Angwarribo family of monkeys, who have but four fingers, and we had not taken on that extra finger, we would have continued to calculate in what is known as the octamal system.

From a mathematical standpoint, it can be shown that the decimal system is not as perfect as some of the others, and that for some purposes the septamal, which only runs up to 7, is better. In that notation 66 would mean six 7's and six 1's, so the addition of 1 more would change it to 100, which would be equal to only 49 in our decimal notation.

You see, 1 added to the 6 in the unit column would change it to 7, so we would have to place a 0 and carry 1 on to the other 6 which in turn becomes a 7, so we place another 0 and carry the 1 to the third column, making it 100, which stands for 49. In this same way, 222 represents 114 — two units, two 7's and two 49's.

Assuming the octamal system to be the popular notation in the Angwarribo days of our four-fingered ancestors, when they counted up to eight and knew nothing about 9's or 10's, how would you write down the year 1906 so as to show the number of years which have elapsed since the Christian era began? It is a pretty problem which will clear the cobwebs from your brain, and introduce you to some elementary principles involved in converting from one number system to another.

106 Annual Picnic

WHEN THEY started off on the great annual picnic, every wagon carried exactly the same number of persons. Half way to the grounds ten wagons broke down, so it was necessary for each remaining wagon to carry one more person.

When they started for home it was discovered that fifteen more wagons were out of commission, so on the return trip there were three persons more in each wagon than when they started out in the morning.

How many people attended the great annual picnic?

THE Convent Problem BY SAM LOYD

107 *How many nuns lived in the convent and what rooms did they occupy?*

THE PROBLEM of the Nuns in the Convent of Mt. Maladetta appears in almost all collections of puzzles, but it is very childish and the answer too weak to satisfy the expectations of solvers.

I remember that the answer was very disappointing when I first saw it many years ago, and I recall the accompanying statement about the problem being of Spanish origin and founded on an incident which occurred many centuries ago. Recently I came into possession of some very old Spanish histories, in one of which I find a brief allusion to the convent of Mt. Maladetta, situated on the mountain of that name, the highest peak of the Pyrenees. Reference is made to the occupancy of that part of the country by the French invaders who were finally defeated and driven out through that famous pass which was the scene of many contentions for over a century.

The direct allusion to the puzzle, however, occurs in the passage which says: "Many of the nuns were carried away by the 'Frank' soldiers, which without doubt gave rise to the familiar problem of the nuns of the convent of Mt. Maladetta."

As no explanation of the puzzle is vouchsafed, and the popular version is so susceptible of double solutions, I take the liberty of presenting it in a form which preserves the spirit of the problem and at the same time eliminates the many other answers.

The convent as shown in the picture was a square three-story structure, with six windows on each side of the upper stories. It is plain to be seen that there are eight rooms on each of the upper floors, which agrees with the requirements of the old story. As the legend goes, the upper floors were used for sleeping apartments. The top floor, having more beds in each of the rooms, accommodated twice as many occupants as the second floor.

The Mother Superior, in accordance with an old rule of the founders, insisted that the occupants must be so divided or arranged that every room should be occupied; there should be twice as many on the top floor as on the second, and there must always be exactly eleven nuns in the six rooms on each of the four sides of the convent. The problem pertains only to the two upper floors, so the ground floor does not have to be considered at all.

Well, it so happened that after the retreat of the French army through the Pyrenees pass, nine of the youngest and most comely nuns were found to have disappeared. It was always believed that they had been captured by the soldiers. Not to distress the Mother Superior, however, the nuns who discovered the loss found that it was possible to conceal the fact by a judicious manipulation or change of the occupants of the rooms.

The nuns managed, therefore, to readjust themselves in such a way that when the Mother Superior made her nightly rounds, every room was found to be occupied; eleven nuns on each of the four sides of the convent; twice as many on the top floor as on the second, and yet the nine nuns were missing. How many nuns were there and how were they arranged?

The merit of the puzzle lies in the paradoxical conditions of the problem, which strikes us at first to be absolutely impossible. Nevertheless it yields so readily to experimental puzzle methods, when one knows there is an answer, that our puzzlists will find it an amusing and instructive lesson.

108 *Show how the merchant measured the wine and water.*

A MERCHANT of Bagdad who catered to the wants of pilgrims who crossed the desert, was once confronted by the following perplexing problem. He was visited by the leader of a caravan, who desired to purchase a store of wine and water. Presenting three ten-gallon vessels, he asked that three gallons of wine be put in the first, three gallons of water in the second, and three of wine and three of water mixed in the third, and three gallons of water be given to each of his thirteen camels.

As water and wine, according to Oriental usage, are sold only in quantities of an even number of gallons, the merchant had only a two and a four gallon measure wherewith to perform a feat which presents some unexpected difficulties. Nevertheless, without resorting to any trick or device, or expedient not used in measuring problems of this type, he dispensed the water from a full hogshead (63 gallons), and the wine from a full barrel (31½ gallons), in the required proportions, without any waste whatever. In how few manipulations can the feat be performed, counting every time liquid is drawn from one receptacle to another as a manipulation?

109 *How many different ways can you spell "Was it a cat I saw?"*

WE CALL attention to Alice's remarkable experiences with the Cheshire cat, which had a way of vanishing into thin air until nothing but its irresistible smile remained. When Alice first saw her feline friend she wanted to know what species of animal it was, and since they always ask questions in Wonderland by writing, she wrote out her query. But because they generally read things backward or up and down in Wonderland, she wrote it as shown in the puzzle. This permits readers to commence and end where they please, just as they should in Wonderland.

The problem is this. In how many different ways can you read Alice's question, "Was it a cat I saw?" Start at any of the W's, spell by moving to adjacent letters until you reach the C, then spell back out to the border again. You may move up and down, left and right.

THE Fighting Fishes of Siam
PRIZE PUZZLE
BY
SAM LOYD

110 *How long will it take one species of fish to vanquish the others?*

THE PEOPLE of Siam are natural born gamblers who would bet their last vestige of clothing upon any event which offers a chance to win or lose. They are not especially belligerent themselves, but they love to witness a fight between any other creatures from toads to elephants. Dog-fights or cocking mains are of daily occurrence and are conducted pretty much according to the recognized lines of civilized countries, but in no other land upon the globe is it possible to witness a fish fight!

They have two kinds of fish which, despite their being very choice food, are raised and valued solely for their fighting qualities. The one is a large white perch known as the king fish, and the other is the little black carp or devil fish. Such antipathy exists between these two species that they attack each other on sight and battle to the death.

A king fish could readily dispose of one or two of the little fish in just a few seconds, but the devil fish are so agile and work together so harmoniously that three of the little fellows would just equal one of the big ones, and they would battle for hours without any results. So cleverly and scientifically do they carry on their line of attack that four of the little fellows would kill a large one in just three minutes and five would administer the *coup de grace* proportionately quicker. (*E.g.*, five would kill one king fish in two minutes and 24 seconds, six in two minutes, and so on.)

These combinations of adverse forces are so accurate and reliable that when a fish tournament is arranged, one can calculate the exact time it will take a given number of one kind to vanquish a certain number of the enemy.

By way of illustration a problem is presented in which four of the king fish oppose thirteen of the little fighters. Who should win? And how long should it take one side to annihilate the other?

[To avoid an ambiguity in Loyd's statement of the problem, it should be made clear that the devil fish always attack single king fish in groups of three or more, and stay with the large fish until he is disposed of. We cannot, for example, assume that while the twelve little fish hold the four large fish at bay, the thirteenth devil fish darts back and forth to finish off the large fish by attacking all of them simultaneously. If we permit fractions, so to speak, of devil fish to be effective then we can reason that if four devils kill a king in three minutes, thirteen devils will finish a king in 12/13 minutes, or four kings in 48/13 minutes (3 minutes, 41 and 7/13 seconds). But this same line of reasoning would lead to the conclusion that twelve devils would kill one king in one minute ,or four kings in four minutes, even without the aid of the thirteenth little fish — a conclusion that clearly violates Loyd's assumption that three little fish are unable to kill one devil fish.—M.G.]

The Chinese Cash Puzzle
BY SAM LOYD

111 What combination of coins will buy the puppy?

THE CHINESE coined money thousands of years before the Christian era, but their inability to comprehend the fundamental principles of currency has led them at times into wild and experimental extravagances. In the Flowery Kingdom large transactions are paid in gold ingots, stamped with the date and name of the banker, but the currency of the country consists of taels or cash of fluctuating value. They made the tael thinner and thinner, until 2,000 of them piled together were less than three inches in height. In like manner the common cash, which is a brass coin with a round, square, or triangular hole in the middle, and worth but little more than a mill of our money, is of variable thickness. The Chinese compute their value by stringing them on a wire, so as to measure their height in chips or bits.

Supposing that eleven coins with round holes are worth 15 bits, while eleven square ones are worth 16 bits, and eleven of triangular shape are worth 17 bits, tell how many round, square, or triangular pieces of cash would be required to purchase that fat little puppy dog, worth 11 bits.

THE CHEESE PROBLEM
—BY—
SAM LOYD

112 *How many pieces of cheese did the soldier produce with six plane cuts?*

THE THEME for a good puzzle can be suggested by anything striking or novel that one chances to see, but the application or proper working out of the scheme may require considerable time and study. Something in the ordinary affairs of life puzzles us a little by its oddity, and the thought naturally occurs, "If this thing perplexed me in its accidental form, when no feature of difficulty was intended, how would it be possible to increase the difficulty by dressing it up in true puzzle form so as to conceal the principle involved?"

The problem must be posed pleasantly, so that the picture aids in explaining the terms and at the same time conceals its real difficulty by imparting what Bret Harte would term a "childlike and bland" simplicity to the whole story. The very name may be utilized to draw attention away from the trick, for, as an old philosopher remarked several centuries before they spoke United States, *"Ars est celare artem,"* by which he meant to inform puzzle-makers that the true art is to conceal the art. Therein lies the main difference between modern and old time puzzles.

Chancing one day to be in an army commissary department when an assistant was portioning out cheese, I was struck by

the ingenious way in which he divided it. The more I thought
it over the more firmly I became convinced that here was a
happy suggestion which would eventually crystalize into puzzle form. I complimented the quartermaster upon the skill of
his assistant, to which he replied: "Oh, that is nothing! You
should see him cut pie!"

The cutting of a piece of pie pertains only to the surface,
going no further than square roots or second powers, as the
mathematician would say. In the portioning of cheese we go
below the surface into cubic equations known as the third
power, for we have to consider the feature of depth.

Can you tell how many pieces are produced by the following
six straight cuts?

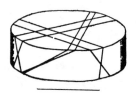

113 The Mixed-up Hats

PUZZLES OF a very interesting nature may arise at any
moment amid the various changes and chances of this mortal
life. George Washington Johnson, the truthful guardian of
the cloak room at a recent fashionable function, vouches for
the correctness of the following problem.

At the close of the festivities there were just six hats left,
but the applicants for these hats were in such a helpless state
of befuddlement that not one of them could produce his hat
check, much less recognize his hat when he saw it. In utter
despair Johnson was compelled to let each man make his own
selection. It so happened that every one of the six took a hat
which did not belong to him. From a puzzler's standpoint it
is interesting to determine the chances against such an event
occurring. If six men each take a hat at random, what is the
probability that no man will get his own hat?

114 Show how the eight crows settled on the corn with no three in a row.

A NOTED ornithologist, describing the habits and sagacity of birds, tells how he witnessed a flock of marauding crows descend upon a corn field and dispose themselves according to established military tactics. Each bird was posted like an army picket, so as to keep an unobstructed view of every one of his companions, and by his motions apparently maintain a noiseless code of signals which kept the entire flock informed of any approaching danger.

Without attempting to investigate the mysteries of crow wireless telegraphy, occasion is taken to show that the statement of the distinguished ornithologist suggests a very pretty problem in the science of picket posting.

Take sixty-four points like the centers of the squares of an 8 x 8 checkerboard, as represented by the hills of sprouting corn in the picture, and the puzzle is to place eight crows on such points that there are no two crows on the same row or diagonal; and so that the man with the gun, going around the field, would find it impossible to get a shot at three birds in a row.

The puzzle is closely allied to my well-known problem of placing eight queens on a chess board so that none is attacked by another, but is an improvement upon the same. There is but one way of performing this feat, while to the other there are twelve different answers.

115 Divide a square piece of paper into two halves which will fit together as shown.

THE STOCKS which secure the head and wrists of the unhappy culprit shown in the picture were made from a square piece of wood divided into two pieces. Like all mathematical problems, the proposition can be worked either way, namely, to make a pair of stocks by dividing a square, or to divide the stocks into halves which will fit together and form a square.

Take a perfectly square piece of paper and, without any

waste, cut it into two pieces which will fit together and form an oblong pair of stocks, with openings as shown for the head and wrists of the culprit. The two pieces forming the stocks can always be refitted back into a perfect square, with the three openings closed. There is a pretty trick connected with the feat of producing holes in the exact positions shown.

116 *Butcher Boy*

MY STORY turns upon an incident told by Ike Reed, of the old horse mart of Johnson & Reed. During the last term of his Presidency General Grant returned from his afternoon drive and in a humorous but somewhat mortified way told Colonel Shadwick, who kept the Willard Hotel, that he had been passed on the road by a butcher cart in a way that made his crack team appear to be standing still. He said he would like to know who owned the horse and if it was for sale.

The horse was readily found and purchased from an unsophisticated German for half of what he would have asked had he known the purchaser was the President of the United States. The horse was of light color and none other than Grant's favorite horse, "Butcher Boy," named after the incident mentioned.

Well, some years later, after the Wall street catastrophe which impaired the finances of the Grant family, Butcher Boy and his mate were sent to the auction rooms of Johnson & Reed, and sold for the sum of $493.68. Mr. Reed said he could have gotten twice as much for them if he had been permitted to mention their owership, but General Grant positively prohibited the fact being made known. "Nevertheless," said Reed, "you come out two percent ahead, for you make 12 percent on Butcher Boy and lose 10 percent on the other."

"I suppose that is the way some people would figure it out," replied the General, but the way he laughed showed that he was better at figures than some people, so I am going to ask our puzzlists to tell me what he got for each horse if he lost 10 percent on one and made 12 percent on the other, but cleared 2 percent on the whole transaction.

117 *Remove the shears without cutting the cord.*

OF COURSE at this late day it would be impossible to correct
the great injustice done to poor Gordius. Nevertheless, as true
blue puzzlists we can condemn the high-handed manner in
which Alexander the Great, competing in a puzzle contest, proceeded to make himself the umpire and awarded himself the
prize for his absurd solution. He established a dangerous prece-
dent and encouraged a kind of puzzle brigandage which is not
extinct to this day. We often find young Alexanders who would
like to solve puzzles according to their own notions and capture prizes after the manner of pirates.

Gordius was an unsophisticated countryman who raised
sheep and grapes, but who by his extreme cleverness became
King of Phrygia. It is told that when he assumed the scepter
he tied his former implements with what is known in history
as the Gordian knot, but in such a peculiar way that the knots
could not be unfastened. The oracles proclaimed that whoever
could untie them would become emperor.

Alexander the Great, it is said, made many ineffectual
attempts to untie some of the knots, but finally becoming
enraged at his want of success, drew his sword and cut the
cord, exclaiming that "such is the common sense way to get a
thing when you want it." Strange that those familiar with the

story and its contemptible climax indorse it with a certain air of assumed pride when they have surmounted some difficulty and exclaim: "I have cut the Gordian knot!"

According to historians and all writers on the subject, the puzzle was a fair and legitimate one, and so accurately and minutely described that many attempts have been made to picture it. Some curious and complicated knots have been invented by imitators of Gordius, and I wonder whether they would be satisfied with the answers to their puzzles if solvers followed the method of Alexander. The only protest against his solution that I can recall, were some clever lines which must be of very ancient origin:

> *A puzzle is not solved, impatient sirs,*
> *By peeping at its answer in a trice —*
> *When Gordius, the plow-boy king of Phrygia,*
> *Tied up his implements of husbandry*
> *In the far-famed knot, rash Alexander*
> *Did not undo by cutting it in twain.*

In presenting this puzzle, I have drawn largely upon encyclopedia lore, but have conformed strictly to the description as I find it. They all agree that the cord was so fixed that no ends could be found and that the implements of husbandry were tied to a staple in the temple of the gods. I have taken Lattimer's intimation that the implements may have been tied separately, and I accept his reference to the pruning shears as being worthy of special illustration.

The puzzle is designed especially for summer outings, and should become popular at the seashore as well as the mountain resorts. It can readily be solved by patience, perserverance, and quiet study. It is a puzzle to be solved in some quiet nook, "far from the maddening crowd."

Get a piece of cord about one yard long, tie the ends together to make an endless piece. Take any kind of ordinary scissors and arrange the string exactly as shown in the picture, only instead of fastening the cord through the staple, throw it, like a necklace, over the head of a young lady, seated in a convenient position, who will aid you to win the crown of Asia by removing the scissors.

SOLUTIONS

Answer 1

The accompanying diagram shows how the French astronomers would locate the new celestial find, which proves to be of such heroic dimensions as to cast the other little stars quite in the shade.

[Loyd's *Cyclopedia* contains no answer to the anagram question. Perhaps he had in mind "MOON STARERS."—M.G.]

Answer 2

The only possible route by which all towns can be visited but once is to take them in the following sequence: Philadelphia to 15, 22, 18, 14, 3, 8, 4, 10, 19, 16, 11, 5, 9, 2, 7, 13, 17, 21, 20, 6, 12, and then to Erie.

Answer 3

The large turkey weighed sixteen pounds, the small one four pounds.

Answer 4

[Loyd does not give his solution to this. Most puzzle books, he says, present a solution in 52 moves, whereas the puzzle can actually be solved in 47. H. E. Dudeney, the British puzzle expert, went Loyd one better by reducing the number to 46. For Dudeney's beautifully symmetric solution, see W. Rouse Ball's *Mathematical Recreations and Essays*, current edition, p. 125.—M.G.]

Answer 5

Out of the 216 equally probable ways the dice may be thrown, you will win on only 91 of them, lose on 125. So your chance of winning at least as much as you bet is 91/216, your chance of losing 125/216.

If the dice always showed different numbers, the game would be a fair one. Suppose all the squares covered with a dollar. The operator would on each roll that showed three different numbers, take in three dollars and pay out three. But on doubles he makes a dollar and on triples he makes two dollars. In the long run, for every dollar wagered by a player, regardless of how he places the money and in what amounts, he can expect to lose about 7.8 cents. This gives the operator a profit of 7.8 percent on each dollar bet.

Answer 6

First cut AB, then put the three pieces together in such a way that cuts CD and EF can be made simultaneously.

The figure below shows how two straight cuts will divide the horseshoe into nine pieces. First cut AB, then put the three pieces together in such a manner that the other three cuts can be made as a single cut.

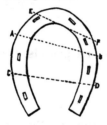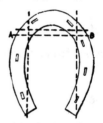

Answer 7

By drawing a line on the bias, from one corner to another, then crossing and paralleling the same, it will be found that 41 vines can be planted, a little over nine feet apart, all well within the fence line.

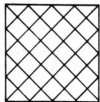

Answer 8

The Greek symbol can be drawn in one continuous line with thirteen turns:

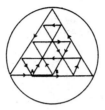

Answer 9

The amusing point of this puzzle is that, play as you will, the "man" can never catch the "rooster" nor the "woman" the "hen," for, as they say in chess or checkers, the rooster "has got the move" on the man, and for the same reason the woman can never get the "opposition" on the hen. But if they reverse matters, the man going after the hen and the woman after the rooster, the chickens are captured easily! One chicken can be taken on the eighth move, the other on the ninth.

Answer 10

[Loyd's answer makes use of the two time intervals given in the problem, but as Ronald C. Read, of Kingston, Jamaica, points out, these time intervals are not really needed in order to solve the problem. Let x be the point (between Bixley and Pixley) where the first question is asked, and y the point (between Pixley and Quixley) where the second question is asked. The distance from x to y, we are told, is 7 miles. Since the distance from x to Pixley is $\frac{2}{3}$ the distance between Bixley and Pixley, and the distance from y to Pixley is $\frac{2}{3}$ the distance between Pixley and Quixley, it follows that the distance between x and y, or 7 miles, is $\frac{2}{3}$ the total distance. This makes the total distance $10\frac{1}{2}$ miles. — M.G.]

Answer 11

[This is the first of many "dissection" problems included in this collection. It may interest the reader to know that there is a proof by David Hilbert that any polygon can be sliced into a finite number of pieces which can be rearranged to form any other polygon of equal area. Such dissections are of little interest, however, unless the number of required pieces is small enough to make the dissection elegant and surprising.

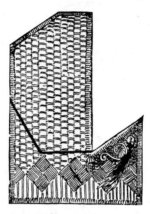

Almost all simple and regular polygons (except the pentagram or five-pointed star which offers formidable difficulties) have been exploited in dissection puzzles of great ingenuity. For a recent and excellent discussion of dissection theory see a series of articles by the mathematics staff of the college, University of Chicago, in *The Mathematics Teacher*, May, October, and December, 1956; February and May, 1957.—M.G.]

Answer 12

The first 18 feet of rope measured by the storekeeper is 3 inches short per yard, or a total of 1 and ½ feet short. Nothing is lost on the last 2 feet since the yardstick is short only at the far end. Therefore the storekeeper gives the sailor 81 and ½ feet of rope, which at 2 cents per foot is worth $1.63. For this he is paid $1.60 (80 feet at 2 cents per foot) with a counterfeit five dollar gold piece. The storekeeper gives the sailor $3.40 in change. This added to his loss of $1.63 worth of rope, makes a total loss of $5.03. The fact that a neighbor changed the gold piece for him has nothing to do with his profit and loss.

Answer 13

The problem has no unambiguous answer unless you know what the dealer paid originally for the bicycle. Since this is not given, the problem cannot be answered in any satisfactory way.

Answer 14

The best method of solving this problem is based on the fact that areas of circles are proportional to the squares of their diameters. If we inscribe a square, ABCD, on a circle the size of the original grindstone, then circle E, inscribed within that square, will have exactly one-half the area of the larger circle.

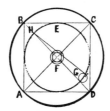

Half the area of the grindstone's hole must now be added to circle E. To do this we inscribe a square on the hole, and within this square we inscribe a circle. The smaller circle will therefore be half the area of the hole. We place the small circle at G so that its diameter forms the side of a right triangle, the base of which is the diameter of circle E. The hypotenuse, HI, will then be the diameter of a circle with an area equal to the combined areas of circle E and the small circle at G. This circle, shown with a dotted line, represents the size of the grindstone after half the stone has been used. Its diameter can be calculated as follows:

The diameter of circle E is the same as the side of the largest square. Knowing the diagonal of this square to be 22 inches, we arrive at the square root of 242 for the side of the square and the diameter of circle E. A similar procedure shows the diameter of the smallest circle to be the square root of 242/49.

The square of the diameter of the dotted circle equals the sum of the squares of the two diameters cited above. So we add 242 to 242/49 to obtain 12100/49, the square root of which is

110/7 or 15 and 5/7. This is the diameter in inches of the dotted circle, and the precise answer to the problem.

Answer 15

Smith must have started out with $99.98, and spent all but $49.99.

Answer 16

The cat wins, of course. It has to make precisely 100 leaps to complete the distance and return. The dog, on the contrary, is compelled to go 102 feet and back. Its thirty-third leap takes it to the 99-foot mark and so another leap, carrying it two feet beyond the mark, becomes necessary. In all, the dog must make 68 leaps to go the distance. But it jumps only two-thirds as quickly as the cat, so that while the cat is making 100 leaps the dog cannot make quite 67.

But Barnum had an April Fool possibility up his sleeve. Suppose that the cat is named Sir Thomas and the dog is female! The phrase "she makes three leaps to his two" would then mean that the dog would go 9 feet while the cat went 4. Thus when the dog finishes the race in 68 leaps, the cat will have traveled only 90 feet and 8 inches.

[This same puzzle stirred up considerable chagrin in London when Henry Dudeney published it in the April 1, 1900, issue of *The Weekly Dispatch*. Dudeney's version, a race between a gardener (female) and a cook (male), will be found in his *Amusements in Mathematics*, problem 428.—M.G.]

Answer 17

Answer 18

In the plumber's problem it will be found that a tank with a square base, twice as wide as it is deep, gives the most economical form. If a cube close to 12.6 feet square holds 2,000 cubic feet, then half that depth would give the required 1,000 cubic feet.

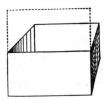

[The exact dimensions of the required tank cannot be stated in rational numbers because they concern one half of a "duplicated cube". Expressed in irrational numbers, the tank would have a length and width equal to the cube root of 2,000, and a depth equal to one-half the cube root of 2,000.—M.G.]

Answer 19

Answer 20

The following illustration shows how the Greek cross may be cut into five pieces which will form two crosses of the

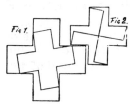

same size. Cut as shown in Fig. 1, and rearrange the small pieces as shown in Fig. 2.

Answer 21

[The original puzzle is impossible to solve except by such skullduggery as turning the 6 and 9 blocks upside down. One of the puzzle's peculiarities is that any such interchange, involving two blocks, immediately converts the puzzle to a solvable one. In fact, any odd number of interchanges has the same effect, whereas an even number leaves the puzzle unsolvable as before. Readers interested in learning something about the interesting mathematical structure underlying this puzzle are referred to the classic analysis by W. W. Johnson and W. E. Story in their article, "Notes on the 15-Puzzle," *American Journal of Mathematics*, Vol. 2, 1879, p. 397f, and to briefer discussions of the puzzle in standard references on recreational mathematics.—M.G.]

The other three problems are solved as follows:

Fig. 1 can be reached in 44 moves: 14, 11, 12, 8, 7, 6, 10, 12, 8, 7, 4, 3, 6, 4, 7, 14, 11, 15, 13, 9, 12, 8, 4, 10, 8, 4, 14, 11, 15, 13, 9, 12, 4, 8, 5, 4, 8, 9, 13, 14, 10, 6, 2, 1.

Fig. 2 can be reached in 39 moves: 14, 15, 10, 6, 7, 11, 15, 10, 13, 9, 5, 1, 2, 3, 4, 8, 12, 15, 10, 13, 9, 5, 1, 2, 3, 4, 8, 12, 15, 14, 13, 9, 5, 1, 2, 3, 4, 8, 12.

The magic square can be produced in 50 moves: 12, 8, 4, 3, 2, 6, 10, 9, 13, 15, 14, 12, 8, 4, 7; 10, 9, 14, 12, 8, 4, 7, 10, 9, 6, 2, 3, 10, 9, 6, 5, 1, 2, 3, 6, 5, 3, 2, 1, 13, 14, 3, 2, 1, 13, 14, 3, 12, 15, 3.

Answer 22

Mary Ann was the sick boy's mother.

Answer 23

If Nobbs can drop a row of potatoes in 40 minutes, it would take him 240 minutes to drop six rows. Since he covers at the same speed, he would complete the six rows in 480 minutes or 8 hours. Hobbs, working on the other six rows, would drop them in 120 minutes (one row per 20 minutes), and cover them in 360 minutes, making a total of 480 minutes or 8 hours.

Each man would have accomplished the same amount of work during the eight hours it took them to complete the field, so each is entitled to $2.50 for his labors.

Answer 24

The mystery of the gold brick is mathematically explained by saying that the new form is really 23 x 25 and 1/23, which still contains 576 square inches.

[For a variety of new "geometrical vanishes" of this sort, see my *Mathematics, Magic and Mystery*, Dover Publications, 1956.—M.G.]

Answer 25

Euclid says: "When two chords of an arc intersect within a circle, the products of the parts of one will be equal to the products of the parts of the other." In the following illustration the surface of the water forms the chord of one arc, and since each part of this chord is 21 inches, the product is 441 inches.

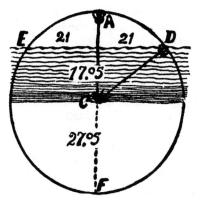

The stem of the lily forms the other intersecting chord, and as its height above the water forms one part of the chord, that part, 10 inches, multiplied by the other part, must be the same as the 441 inches obtained by the parts of the other chord. So divide 441 by 10, and we get 44.1 inches as the other part of that chord. Adding the 10 and the 44.1, we get 54.1 for the total length of the chord from A to F, which is the diameter of the circle. This we must halve to get the radius, 27.05, but as the flower stood ten inches above the surface of the water, we must deduct that ten inches to obtain the depth of the lake —17.05 inches.

Answer 26

If you draw one of the diagonals on a rectangular sheet of paper, then roll the sheet into a cylinder, the diagonal will form a spiral around the cylinder. In other words, a spiral around a column may be regarded as the hypotenuse of a right triangle. In this case, it is a right triangle wrapped four times around the column. The base of this triangle is four times the circumference of the cylinder (*pi* times the diameter times four), which proves to be a negligible fraction above 300 feet. This is also the height of the tower, which is just a coincidence because the height does not enter at all into the solution of the problem.

Nor do we have to consider the length of the stairway. For if pickets are a foot apart on the base of a right triangle, the same number will be the same distance apart on the hypotenuse regardless of how long it is. Since the base of our right triangle is 300 feet, there would be 300 steps on the circular stairs.

Answer 27

In that trading chickens puzzle it is plain to any farmer that a cow is worth twenty-five chickens, and a horse is worth sixty. They must have already selected five horses and seven cows, worth 475 chickens, and since they had just enough to trade for seven more cows, they had 175 chickens left, which would make 650 in all.

Answer 28

There are 416 ways of doing this trick of which the shortest route is O-P, D-C, E-F, H-G, I-J, L-K, N-M and A-B; but as there are several million ways of *not* doing it, such a small matter as 416 routes may have been overlooked.

[The reader must not take seriously Loyd's jibes at the great

Euler, who, as Loyd of course knew, was concerned only with the seven bridges, and whose famous paper was the first published analysis of a topological problem.—M.G.]

Answer 29

The Fifth Regiment will be passed by the other nineteen regiments, leaving the chess-player with 1,370 men in his regiment. It will require eighteen more weeks, gaining 30 each week, to bring this regiment above the 1,900 now required as a quota; so 37 weeks, with 1,900 men is the correct answer.

Answer 30

Mathematicians and puzzlists who revel in the mysteries of permutations, have computed that no less than 92,160 different fob chains can be made from four coins and the pendant eagle, so that no two are alike.

It is evident that the large coin could be suspended from any one of the five holes, and with either side toward you, which would make ten possible changes. As the nickel can be placed in eight positions, these two coins alone would represent eighty combinations, which, multiplied by the six positions of the penny, and again by the four changes of the dime and the two positions of the eagle, show that in the order of size in which the coins are now strung there could be 3,840 changes. Since there are twenty-four different strings of coins to be made by merely changing the order of the coins, 3,840 times 24 gives 92,160 as the correct answer to the puzzle.

Answer 31

The feat can be performed in 17 trips.

We begin with ABCD (the men) and abcd (the girls) all on shore. The following chart is self-explanatory:

	Shore	Island	Other side
1.	A B C D c d	o	a b
2.	A B C D b c d	o	a
3.	A B C D d	b c	a
4.	A B C D c d	b	a

(Now the men begin to do some rowing.)

5.	C D c d	b	A B a
6.	B C D c d	b	A a
7.	B C D	b c d	A a
8.	B C D d	b c	A a
9.	D d	b c	A B C a
10.	D d	a b c	A B C
11.	D d	b	A B C a c
12.	B D d	b	A C a c
13.	d	b	A B C D a c
14.	d	b c	A B C D a
15.	d	o	A B C D a b c
16.	c d	o	A B C D a b
17.	o	o	A B C D a b c d

[There are other methods of solving the problem in 17 moves, but as Henry Dudeney explains in his *Amusements in Mathematics,* this solution involves the fewest "gettings in" and "gettings out." When only three couples are involved, the island is not necessary, but four or more couples require an island in order to meet the problem's conditions.—M.G.]

Answer 32

The first girl was just 638 days old, and the boy twice as much, namely 1,276 days. The next day the youngest girl will be 639 days old, and her new recruit 1,915 days, total, 2,554 days, which doubles that of the first boy, who having gained one day, will be 1,277 days old. The next day the boy, being 1,278 days old, brings his big brother, who is 3,834 days old, so their combined ages amount to 5,112 days, just twice the ages of the girls who will now be 640 and 1,916, or 2,556.

The next day, the girls gaining one day each, will represent 2,558 days, which added to 7,670 days of the last recruit, brings their sum total to 10,228 days, just twice that of the two boys, which, with the two points added for the last day, would be increased to 5,114 days.

We arrive at the 7,670 days as follows. The young lady having reached her twenty-first birthday, 21 times 365 equals 7,665 plus 4 days for four leap years, and the extra one day which is the day of her twenty-first birthday.

Those who gave the boy's age as 3½ years overlooked the feature of increasing the ages of the pupils from day to day.

Answer 33

There is but one way to perform the feat in fourteen turns, as shown, although there are a thousand and one routes calling for just one extra turn.

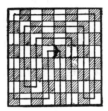

Answer 34

The combined pulling power of the four stout boys just equals that of the five plump sisters. As the second sketch shows the slim twins to be equal to a stout boy and two plump girls, we will at once simplify matters in the third illustration by changing the two slim twins for their equivalent in pulling power, so we substitute the fat boy and two plump girls.

By this change we now have in the third picture five plump sisters and one stout boy opposed to one plump girl and four stout boys. Then cancel off five plump girls from one side and four stout boys from the other, because the first sketch shows these two groups to be equal. This leaves one plump girl on the right opposed to one boy, which proves that the left hand team should win in the third sketch as it has one-fifth of a boy's strength more than the other team.

Answer 35

The cubical area of a ball may be considered as made up of a great number of small pyramids, with apexes meeting at the center of the ball, and their bases representing the surface. We know that the volume of a pyramid is equal to its base multiplied by one-third its height. Therefore, the volume of the sphere is equal to the sum of the bases multiplied by one-third of the constant height—in this case, the surface of the sphere multiplied by one-third of the radius. If this volume is to be equal in number to the surface, it follows that one-third of the radius is unity. Therefore, the radius is 3 and the diameter of the ball 6 inches.

Answer 36

In this remarkable problem we find that the lake contained exactly 11 acres, therefore the approximate answer of "nearly 11 acres" is not sufficiently correct. This definite answer is worked out by the Pythagorean law, which proves that on any right-angle triangle the square of the longest side is equal to the sum of the squares of the other two sides.

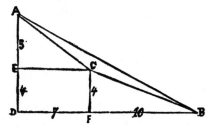

In the illustration ABD represents our triangle, AD being 9 acres long and BD 17, because 9 x 9 equals 81, which added to 17 x 17 (289) equals the 370 acres of the largest field. AEC is a right-angle triangle, and the square of 5 (25) added to the square of 7 (49) shows that the square on AC equals 74. CBF also is a right-angle triangle. The square of its sides, 4 and 10, prove the square estate on BC to equal 116 acres. The area of our triangle ADB is clearly half of 9 x 17, which equals 76.5 acres. Since the areas of the oblong and two triangles can plainly be seen to be 65.5, we deduct the same from 76.5 to prove that the lake contains exactly 11 acres.

Answer 37

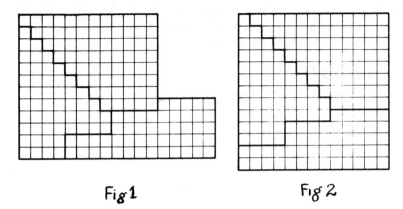

Fig 1   Fig 2

Answer 38

The married names of the three brides are Kitty Brown, Nellie Jones, and Minnie Robinson. Kitty weighed 122, Nellie 132, and Minnie 142 pounds.

Answer 39

Each earring stone was five karats, making each worth $2,500, or $5,000 for both. The stones of differing size were one karat (worth $100) and seven karats (worth $4,900), making their combined worth also $5,000.

Answer 40

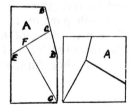

The best answer requires only two straight cuts and the turning over of one piece, a practical piece of carpentering which some of the followers of Euclid did not think of.

It makes no difference if the angle from D to B be more or less acute. Simply draw a line from the center of the left side to the middle of line BD. Then draw a perpendicular line from corner G to line EC. Turn over piece A and the three pieces will form the square as shown.

Answer 41

```
749)  638897  (853
      5992
      ────
       3969
       3745
       ────
       2247
       2247
```

Answer 42

The conversation occurred at 9:36 A.M., because one-quarter of the time from midnight would be 2 hours and 24 minutes, which added to half the time till midnight (7 hours and 12 minutes), equals 9:36.

Were it not for the fact that McGuire bid Clancy good morning, showing that their conversation took place in the A.M., it might be assumed that the time was P.M., and 7:12 P.M. would be an equally correct answer.

Answer 43

If the minute hand goes twelve times faster than the hour hand, then they will meet eleven times during every 12-hour period. By taking the eleventh part of 12 hours for our constant, we find there will be a meeting of hands every 65 and 5/11 minutes, or every 65 minutes, 27 and 3/11 seconds. The hands will next come together, therefore, at 5 minutes, 27 and 3/11 seconds past 1 o'clock.

The following table shows the time of the eleven meetings of the hands during every 12-hour period.

12: 00: 00
1: 05: 27 and 3/11
2: 10: 54 and 6/11
3: 16: 21 and 9/11
4: 21: 49 and 1/11
5: 27: 16 and 4/11
6: 32: 43 and 7/11
7: 38: 10 and 10/11
8: 43: 38 and 2/11
9: 49: 05 and 5/11
10: 54: 32 and 8/11

[Now that you are acquainted with the technique of solving problems of this type, you may wish to tackle this seemingly more difficult one. Suppose that a clock has three hands, all exactly together at noon. The third hand, of course, is a second hand. When will be the next meeting of the *three* hands?

Actually, with the help of the table above and an insight that will provide you with a shortcut, the problem is much easier than you might at first think—M.G.]

Answer 44

There were three totally blind serpents and three with both eyes sound.

Answer 45

The black pieces of paper are nothing but a delusion and a snare. The pieces are placed to make a little white horse in the center as shown.

It was this trick of the white horse of Uppington which popularized the slang expression: "Oh, but that is a horse of another color!"

Answer 46

There are many simple ways of performing the feat in fifteen to eighteen moves, but the following plan in fourteen moves, returning to starting point, seems to be the best possible answer:

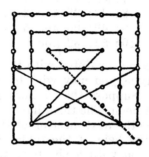

Answer 47

In giving the answer to the necklace puzzle it may be said that any jeweler, as well as ninety-nine out of a hundred mathematicians, would say that to solve the necklace puzzle would be to open the smaller links at the ends of the twelve pieces, which, it may readily be seen, would reduce the cost to $1.80. The correct answer, however, is arrived at by opening the ten links on those two small five-link pieces, on the right and left sides, which have three small and two large links each. To open and mend those ten links so as to bring the chain into an endless necklace would cost just $1.70, which is the cheapest possible answer.

Answer 48

In the puzzle of the pasture field it becomes necessary to figure upon the daily growth of grass. We were told that the cow eats as much as the goat and the goose. Therefore, if the cow and goat eat the stock of standing grass added to 45 days' growth in 45 days, it is plain that two goats and a goose would take the same time. Since a goat and goose would be twice as long, we see that one goat would take 90 days, and that the goose could just keep up with the-growing grass. Therefore, if the cow eats 1/60 of the stock per day, and the goat 1/90, together they would eat 1/36. Thus the cow and goat would eat up the standing crop in 36 days, while the goose devotes the same time to taking care of the daily growth.

Answer 49

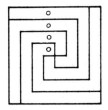

Answer 50

Mrs. O'Toole weighs 135 pounds, the baby 25 pounds, the dog 10 pounds.

Answer 51

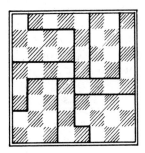

Answer 52

The ancient problem of measuring four quarts with a five and a three quart pitcher, can be solved in six moves.

1. Fill the large pitcher.
2. Fill the small pitcher from the large one, leaving two quarts in the large.
3. Pour the contents of the small pitcher back into the barrel.
4. Transfer the two quarts to the small pitcher.
5. Fill the large pitcher from the barrel.
6. Fill the small pitcher from the large one, leaving four quarts in the large.

On the second problem, a bit of elementary algebra will tell you that 26 gallons of Mountain Dew must contain 24 and 8/17 gallons of applejack and 1 and 9/17 gallons of cider in order to cost $21.06 at the prices given. To measure this mixture in the fastest possible way, the following steps are necessary:

1. Fill both measures with applejack.
2. Empty the applejack barrel into the keg.
3. Empty both measures back into the applejack barrel.
4. Transfer two gallons from the keg to the applejack barrel.
5. Transfer two gallons of cider from the cider barrel to the keg.
6. Fill both measures with the mixture now in the keg. This will leave a mixture in the keg that contains 1 and 9/17 gallons of cider.
7. Fill the keg from the applejack barrel.

Answer 53

There are infinite pairs of numbers which have the same sum and product. If one number is a, the other number can always be found simply by dividing a by a—1. For example: 3 times 1½ equals 4½, and 3 plus 1½ also equals 4½.

Answer 54

In the original Chinese switch-word puzzle they use a sentence of twelve words, because in the Chinese language every word is represented by a specific sign. In the present Americanized version of the puzzle the sentence must be translated or represented by a twelve-letter word, one letter on each block.

Few solvers caught my intimation that there was a peculiarly appropriate word, or who took their "queues" from the Chinese interpreters. The lucky word "interpreting" runs it right off the reel in twelve plays without any "drilling," as the railroad men term it.

Answer 55

The best player claimed that because he beat No. 4, he did not lose. But No. 4, having beaten No. 3, said that he could not be held for the game, while No. 3 maintained that in partnership with No. 2 he had beaten No. 1, and therefore, according to contract, could not be called the loser.

There are other complications which open up different lines of argument. Since No. 4 came in as a free-lance, he is not bound by any private agreements; so, when he made four to the low man's two, he put on his hat and coat and went home. No. 1 then had to live up to his agreement, so, as he had secured but five balls to his opponents' six, the defeat which No. 3 would have sustained was transferred over to No. 1, who should pay for the game.

But there is another view of the matter which would seem to reverse that verdict. Nos. 3 and 2 have scored against No. 1 by special agreement, but as No. 1 has beaten No. 4, he is relieved of all responsibility. Since Nos. 2, 3, and 4 played upon even terms, without any agreement, No. 3 loses.

[The problem obviously is a semantic one with no clear answer. As soon as the fourth player entered the game it became necessary for the players to come to some kind of advance agreement on the meaning of the word "loser." Because they came to no such agreement, the word has no precise meaning under the circumstances. But like the old question of whether the hunter did or didn't "go around" the squirrel, Loyd's pool problem can provoke amusing arguments.—M.G.]

Answer 56

Fifty points can be scored by knocking down the dummies marked 25, 6, and 19.

Answer 57

The number of men when Casey was alive must be a multiple of 2, 3, 4, 5, 6, 7, 8, 9, and 10. We take the least common multiple, 2520, then subtract 1 to get the number of members without Casey. This could be the answer were it not for the catch phrase, "as eleven would not do." Since 2,519 is divisible by 11 we have to go to the next highest multiple, 5040, then subtract 1 to get 5039. Since this is not divisible by 11, and since higher multiples will give answers above 7,000, we conclude that 5039 is the only correct answer.

Answer 58

Three 12-inch napkins will cover a 15 and $\frac{1}{4}$ inch square table. Place one squarely on one corner and the others will easily cover the remainder.

Answer 59

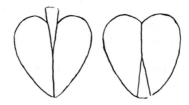

Answer 60

It can readily be shown that if the apples sold for 1/3 of a penny and 1/2 of a penny, they would average 5/6 for two, or 25/60 of a penny per apple. Since they were closed out at a rate of five apples for 2 pence, which is the same as 2/5 or 24/60 of a penny per apple, then 1/60 of a penny was lost on each apple.

We know that 7 pence was lost, so we multiply 60 by 7 to get 420, the number of original apples of which each lady had one-half. Mrs. Jones should have received 105 pence for her 210 apples, but because she received half the proceeds of the entire sale at five apples for 2 pence (that is, 84 pence), she lost 21 pence. Mrs. Smith, who should have received 70 pence for her apples, actually got 85 pennies.

Answer 61

If we convert the odds to probability fractions, we find that the probability of winning is 1/3 for the hippo, 2/5 for the rhino. Since the three probabilities must add to 1, we conclude that the giraffe's probability of winning is 4/15, or odds of 11 to 4 against him.

The answer to the second problem is that the giraffe would beat the hippo by 23/64 of a mile. Assuming that the giraffe ran 2 miles in one hour, then the rhino would run 1 and 7/8 miles in the same time, or 2 miles in 16/15 hours. While the rhino ran these 2 miles the hippo would cover 1 and 3/4 miles in the same time, or 105/64 miles in 1 hour. Since 2 miles is the same as 128/64 miles, we have only to subtract the 105/64 to obtain our answer. The answer will be the same, of course, if we assign any other speed to the giraffe.

Answer 62

Five two-cent stamps, fifty ones, and eight fives will cost exactly $1.00.

Answer 63

Curiously, the answer proves to be identical with the number of square feet to an acre, namely 43,560. This number of rails will form a three-rail fence that will inclose a square of exactly 43,560 acres.

Answer 64

There are one or two ways of varying the answer, but the principle involved is always the same in producing the required result.

He loses seven single francs in succession, then loses three 7-franc bets and wins four 7-franc ventures, which makes his losses and gains equal.

He then wins twice on 49, loses five times on the same number, then wins seven times on 343.

He now loses three times on 2,401 and wins four times, then wins twice on 16,807 and loses five times, and finally wins seven times on the limit of 117,649. In all he has won 869,288 francs and lost 91,511, which leaves him just 777,777 francs ahead of the game.

Answer 65

The secret turns upon placing the first egg exactly in the center of the napkin as shown in the square diagram. Then, no matter where your opponent places an egg, duplicate his play on the opposite side in a direct line through egg No. 1. The numbers given illustrate the beginning of a game, proceeding in regular order of play.

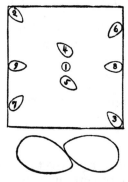

The placing of the first egg in the center would not win if it were simply laid on the table, for, owing to the oval form of the egg, the second player might place an egg in close proximity to the conical end, as shown in the last illustration. This play could not be duplicated.

The only way to win, therefore, as discovered by the great navigator, is to flatten one end of the first egg played to make it stand erect.

Answer 66

It may be said that the peasants as well as some of our puzzlists experimented for some time before a mirror until they hit upon the answer of nine sheep and nine goats. The product, 81, becomes 18 in the mirror which is the total number in the flock.

Answer 67

The first leg of the triangle was sailed in 80 minutes, the second in 90, the last in 160, making a total time of 5½ hours. [This can be solved algebraically by dividing the course into 12 equal parts, letting x stand for the first four parts, x plus 10 for the middle four, and y for the last four. Our data (expressed in minutes) now permits us to formulate the following two equations from which it is not difficult to determine the values of x and y.

$$\frac{x}{4} + x + 10 + y = 270$$

$$\frac{y}{4} + x + 10 + x = 210$$

—M.G.]

Answer 68

Harold's thirteen squares of men were squares with 180 men on the side, making a total of 421,200 men. With the addition of Harold the number becomes 421,201 which will form one large square with 649 men on the side.

[In borrowing this problem from Henry Dudeney, the British puzzle expert, Loyd modified it considerably to make it both easier as well as more plausible historically. Dudeney's version, to be found in his *Amusements in Mathematics*, has 61 squares of men instead of 13. Lest you be tempted to work on this problem, let me hasten to say that the lowest possible number of men in this case is 3,119,882,982,860,264,400 (each square consisting of 226,153,980 men on the side). With the addition of Harold, they could then form a single square with 1,766,319,049 men on the side. The general problem, Dudeney says, of which this is a special case, was first proposed by Fermat although it has come to be known as the "Pellian equation."—M.G.]

Answer 69

The fifty thousand readers who reported "There is no possible way" had all solved the puzzle, for that is the sentence that makes a round trip tour of the planet!

Answer 70

A cube 17.299 inches on the side, and a cube 25.469 inches on the side, have a combined volume (21,697.794418608 cubic inches) exactly equal to the combined volume of twenty-two cubes each 9.954 inches on the side. Therefore the green and black teas must have been mixed in the proportion of 17,299^3 to 25,469^3.

Answer 71

The problem calls for a number which when cubed will give a square number. This happens to be the case with any number which is itself a square. The smallest square (aside from 1) is 4, so the monument might consist of 64 small cubes (4 x 4 x 4) which would stand on the center of an 8 x 8 square. This, however, will not fit the proportions shown in the sketch.

We therefore try the next highest square, 9, which gives us a monument of 729 cubes standing on a 27 x 27 square. This is the correct answer for it is the only one which agrees with the illustration.

Answer 72

The large box must be 13.856 inches on the side and the small one 6.928 inches. The two together measure 20.784 inches or 1.732 feet, which at $5 per running foot would be $8.66. The two boxes together contain a trifle more than 2,992 cubic inches or 1.732 cubic feet. At the rate of $5 per cubic foot this would also amount to $8.66.

Answer 73

That odd little sleight-of-hand performance with the four empty and four full glasses can readily be remembered by the following rule: One long move, two short ones, then one long one. First move 2 and 3 to the extreme end; then fill the gap with 5 and 6. Fill gap with 8 and 2; then finish with 1 and 5.

Answer 74

For the benefit of those who were unable to escape the endless whirlpool of numbers that held them in its vortex, we say that the shortest escape is by means of a curious backward-forward sequence along a single diagonal.

The moves are: SW to 4, SW to 6, NE to 6, NE to 2, NE to 5, SW to 4, SW to 4, SW to 4, then a bold strike NW to liberty!

Answer 75

The entire party can be ferried across the stream in seventeen trips as follows:

1. Mr. and Mrs. C. cross over.
2. Mr. C. returns alone.
3. Mr. C. takes over a lady.
4. Mr. C. returns with his wife.
5. Mr. C. takes over another lady.
6. Mr. C. returns alone.
7. The two gentlemen cross over.
8. Gentleman and wife return.
9. Mr. and Mrs. C. cross over.
10. Gentleman and wife return.
11. Two gentleman cross over.
12. Mr. C. comes back alone.
13. Mr. C. takes lady over.
14. Mr. and Mrs. C. return.
15. Mr. C. takes lady over.
16. Mr. C. returns alone.
17. Mr. C. and wife go over.

Answer 76

The following diagram shows how the 13 x 13 quilt can be divided into eleven smaller squares, the least number of square pieces which it will divide into without destroying the checkered pattern. It proved to be a difficult puzzle, and those who discovered the correct answer found that there was a certain mathematical principle involved which held them close to the rules of square roots.

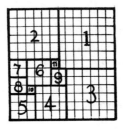

Answer 77

The course can be run in twenty-six shots by using a 150-yard drive and a 125-yard approach. The shots are made as follows:

> 150 yards: 1 drive
> 300 yards: 2 drives
> 250 yards: 2 approaches
> 325 yards: 3 drives, 1 approach back
> 275 yards: 1 drive, 1 approach
> 350 yards: 4 approaches, 1 drive back
> 225 yards: 3 approaches, 1 drive back
> 400 yards: 1 drive, 2 approaches
> 425 yards: 2 drives, 1 approach

Answer 78

There are many ways of solving this puzzle mathematically, but for simplicity's sake, I should tell the poor Danish sailors, who know nothing about square root, to subtract one-half the diagonal from one-quarter the distance around the flag. The distance around the flag being exactly 25 feet, and the diagonal being 9.01388, we must take 4.50694 from 6.25 to obtain 1.74306 feet, the breadth of the cross.

Answer 79

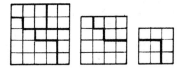

Answer 80

If the broker weighed the goods with a pound weight one ounce too heavy, he got 17 ounces for a pound. When he sold them by a weight one ounce light he gave 15 ounces for a pound, and had two ounces over. If these two ounces were sold at the same price, so as to make $25 by cheating, it is plain that the two ounces represent 2/15 of what he paid for the whole and charged for the 15 ounces. One-fifteenth being worth $12.50, fifteen-fifteenths, or the whole, would be $187.50, which, if there was no question of commission, would be what he paid for the goods.

We find, however, that he received 2 percent from the seller, $3.75, and $4.25 from the purchaser, making $8 brokerage in addition to $25, by cheating. Now, if he had dealt honestly, he would have paid for 17 ounces, which, to be exact, would have been $199.21875. His brokerage for buying and selling would therefore only be $7.96875, so he has made an additional 3 and 1/8 cents by cheating. As the story said that he made exactly $25 by cheating, we must reduce the $187.50, price so that his two cheatings will amount to just $25.

Now, as 3 and 1/8 cents is exactly 1/801 part of $25.03125, we must reduce $187.50 by its 1/801 part, which will bring it down to $187.27, so that he will make just $25 and the .0006 of a cent by cheating. To such as wish to be very exact, I would suggest that the seller be paid $187.2659176029973125 less the 2 percent brokerage of $3.745 plus.

Answer 81

In answering this old chestnut we must take into account the fact that gold is always weighed by troy weight while feathers are weighed in avoirdupois units. In such cases the time honored maxim of "A pound's a pound the world over" will not apply.

Six dozen dozen pounds of feathers weigh 864 pounds avoir-dupois, while 72 pounds troy of gold equal only 59 pounds, 3 ounces, and 407½ grains. Since 864 pounds can be expressed as 863 pounds, 15 ounces, and 437½ grains, we have only to subtract 59 pounds, 3 ounces, and 407½ grains to obtain 804 pounds, 12 ounces, and 30 grains. This is our answer expressed in avoirdupois units.

The average person has no conception of the relation between the two systems. Some believe that the pound weighs the same in both, but in one system it is divided into 16 ounces, in the other into 12. More people, however, think that the ounces are the same, but the avoirdupois pound weighs 16 ounces whereas the troy pound weighs only 12. Neither is correct. The connecting link between the two systems is the fact that a pound avoirdupois weighs 7,000 grains, whereas a pound troy weighs only 5,760 grains.

Answer 82

The quarrelsome neighbors made their paths as shown in the accompanying sketch.

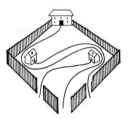

Answer 83

That honest milkman began with five gallons of milk in can No. 2 and eleven gallons of water in can No. 1. Performing the operations described will result in six gallons of water and two of milk in the first can, five gallons of water and three of milk in the second can.

Answer 84

In the puzzle of the young stenographer's salary, she gains $12.50 the first year, but after that loses steadily. Some puzzlists fall into the error of adding the whole of each raise in a lump sum at the end of every six months, whereas the salary was raised each time to a yearly basis of $25 better, which is only an improvement of $12.50 every six months. Of course a raise of $100 per year would give the clerk in five years, $600 plus $700 plus $800 plus $900 plus $1,000, equaling $4,000. Instead of which the clerk loses $437.50 by her own plan, as follows:

		Yearly basis
First six months	$300.00	$600
Second six months	312.50	625
Third six months	325.00	650
Fourth six months	337.50	675
Fifth six months	350.00	700
Sixth six months	362.50	725
Seventh six months	375.00	750
Eighth six months	387.50	775
Ninth six months	400.00	800
Tenth six months	412.50	825

Answer 85

The mother's age is 29 years and 2 months. Tommy's age is 5 years and 10 months, and the father is 35 years old.

Answer 86

The three doublets are: twice in the 25 ring, twice in the 20 ring, twice in the 3.

Answer 87

Here is a simple, common sense method of getting at the answer, which differs from the way others might tackle it. According to the puzzle method of working backward, I should analyze it from the last payment by asking: "The last payment of $1,000 is 105 per cent of what sum of money?" Dividing $1,000 by 105 shows that $952.3809 with 5 per cent interest would be the amount of the last payment.

Going backward again to the previous payment we ask what sum must $1,952.3809 have been 105 per cent of. Divide again by 105, and we get $1,859.4103. Add the other payment of

$1,000 and we get $2,723.2479 as the previous amount. Add $1,000 to make it $3,723.2479, and another division carries it back to $3,545.9503. Add $1,000 once more and another division will give $4,329.4764 as the balance to bear interest, after the first $1,000 payment. So $5,329.4764 was the actual value received for the property, because that sum drawing interest at 5 per cent would just meet the six $1,000 payments according to agreement.

Answer 88

The feat can be performed in 19 steps as follows: go to rung 1, then back to the ground, and proceed to steps 1, 2, 3, 2, 3, 4, 5, 4, 5, 6, 7, 6, 7, 8, 9, 8, 9.

Answer 89

In the sketch illustrating that bottle puzzle, only two burglars were in view, but it does not take a Sherlock Holmes long to prove that there were three burglars in this gang. There were twenty-one pints of wine, twelve large bottles, and twelve small bottles to be divided, and three is the only number which will go evenly into those quantities.

One burglar takes three full quarts, one empty quart, one full pint and three empty pints. Each of the others takes two full quarts and two empty ones, three full pints and one empty one, so each man gets three and a half quarts of wine, and four large and four small bottles.

Answer 90

In the election puzzle, add the pluralities to the total vote and divide by the number of candidates. The quotient will be the vote of the successful one, from which the votes of the others can be ascertained by subtraction. The counts were 1,336, 1,314, 1,306, and 1,263.

Answer 91

This puzzle game proved replete with opportunities for surprises and fine points of play. The first player should score seven boxes by beginning with a line from G to H. If the second player then marks from J to K, the first will score two boxes by marking from K to O and P to L, and will then play a waiting move, L to H, instead of scoring two more boxes. The other player now scores the two boxes by marking G to K, then is compelled to make a play which gives the first player five others.

If, after the first player marks G-H, the second marks D-H, the first marks C-G, B-F, E-F, then the waiting play M-N, he is sure to score four more boxes. It is this clever technique of giving away two boxes in order to get more that constitutes the pretty feature of the game.

[Known to American school children as "Dots and Squares," this is probably the simplest, most widely played example of a topological game. It can be played of course on rectangular fields of varying size and shape. The square field of nine dots is easily analyzed, but the 16-dot board involved in Loyd's puzzle is complex enough to offer a real challenge. I know of no published analysis of a winning strategy for the first or second player (it cannot end in a draw because of the odd number of boxes).

In 1951 Richard Haynes, of 1215 E. 20th Street, Tulsa, Oklahoma, invented an interesting three-dimensional version of this game which he titled "Q-bicles." A set of printed sheets for playing Q-bicles can be obtained by sending one dollar to Mr. Haynes. The game can also be played on lattice points that form triangular or hexagonal two-dimensional cells.—M.G.]

Answer 92

Geertring bought 1 little pig for 1 shilling, and her husband, who must have been Cornelius, bought 8 hogs for 8 shillings each. Caterun bought 9 for 9 shillings each, while her husband Claas bought 12 hogs for 12 shillings each. Anna bought 31 large hogs for 31 shillings each, while her good man Hendrick bought 32 hogs at 32 shillings apiece.

Answer 93

To solve the puzzle in the fewest possible number of pieces, first clip off the little triangles 1 and 2 and pack them into the center. Then cut the zig-zag steps, move piece No. 4 down one step, and the four pieces fit together to make a perfect square.

[It is ironic that in the very puzzle in which Loyd castigates the "smart Alec" who thinks he knows everything, the old master himself fell into a grave error. As Henry Dudeney carefully explains (*Amusements in Mathematics*, Problem No. 150), only rectangles with sides in certain proportions can be transformed into squares by the stairstep method. In this case the rectangle's sides have a ratio of 3 to 4, which does not permit a stairstep transformation. A neat five-piece solution is given by Dudeney. No four-piece solution has ever been found.

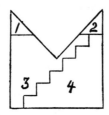

Even Loyd's older mitre puzzle, that of cutting the mitre into four pieces of the same size and shape, can be solved only by the unsatisfying assumption that pieces bearing the same letter (Fig. 1 below) are joined at their corners and can there-

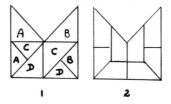

fore be called one piece! Loyd also published the more legitimate eight-piece dissection shown in Fig. 2.—M.G.]

Answer 94

Fourteen straight lines will solve the puzzle as shown below.

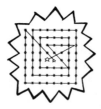

Answer 95

1. Back the R engine far out to the right.
2. Run the R engine on to switch.
3. Run L engine with three cars out to the right.
4. R engine back to the main track.
5. R engine out to the left, with three cars to left of switch.
6. L engine on to switch.
7. R engine and cars to right.
8. R engine pulls seven cars to left.
9. L engine runs to main track.
10. L engine backs to train.
11. L engine pulls five cars to right of switch.
12. L engine backs rear car on to switch.
13. L engine draws four cars to right.
14. L engine backs four cars to left.
15. L engine goes alone to right.
16. L engine backs to switch.
17. L engine pulls car from switch to track.
18. L engine backs to left.
19. L engine goes forward with six cars.
20. L engine backs rear car on to switch.
21. L engine goes to right with five cars.
22. L engine backs five cars to left.
23. L engine goes to right with one car.
24. L engine backs to switch.
25. L engine goes to right with two cars.
26. L engine backs to left of switch.
27. L engine draws seven cars to right of switch.
28. L engine backs end car on to switch.
29. L engine goes to right with six cars.
30. R train backs to right.
31. R train picks up its four cars and skips.
32. L train backs to switch.
33. L train picks up its third car and goes on its way rejoicing.

Answer 96

Duck shooting at Buzzard's Bay is solved by changing the position of two ducks, as shown. This forms five rows of four-in-line and places one duck in Grover's game bag.

Answer 97

Mrs. Jones was the daughter of Smith and the niece of Brown, so there were but four persons. $100 was contributed, $92 spent, and each received $2 in the distribution.

Answer 98

The crazy clock will next show the correct time at 5 minutes, 27 and 3/11 seconds past 7.

[Loyd does not explain how to obtain this answer, but we cannot resist pointing out how simple the problem is once you have worked out the previous clock puzzle titled "The Time Problem." Let us suppose that the bewitched clock actually has four hands—one pair moving properly, the other pair reversed. The reversed hands will then show a correct time only when they coincide with the other pair— hour hand on hour hand, minute hand on minute hand. Since one pair of hands is reversed, we may regard the two hands which point at 12 as an hour hand and a minute hand, then ask when these two hands will next coincide. This of course is precisely the question of the previous clock problem, the answer to which is 5 minutes, 27 and 3/11 seconds past 12. In this case, however, it gives us only the position of the bewitched *minute* hand.

We now turn our attention to the pair of hour hands which point to 6 at the outset and we find an analogous situation. Since one of these hands is moving like a minute hand, the two will meet again the same distance beyond 6 as the other pair will meet beyond 12. Hence the answer cited above.—M.G.]

Answer 99

When Smith and his wife first met, he was three times her age, but on that leap-year day of 1896 she was the age he was when first they met. Mathematicians and others deep in astrology and the occult sciences demonstrated that Tom was fifteen and his sweetheart five when first they met, so on the 29th of February, 1896, she would be fifteen and he would be twenty-five. So, when she is forty-five he will be fifty-five, which would make their combined ages amount to the required century run.

Some of our scientists, however, who reasoned that Tom was twenty-five on the 29th of February, 1896, fell into the error, as did Tom himself, in thinking that 1900, which came four years after, was a leap year, which would make Tom just 29 years old. By some odd freak of the calendar, as explained by the dream books, 1900 was not a leap year. The next leap year did not occur until 1904, on which eventful occasion Tom was 33.

Answer 100

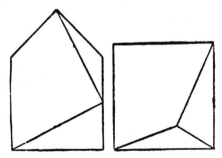

Answer 101

By taking the best possible advantage of the crescent form of the moon, 21 pieces of green cheese can be cut for the hungry mountaineers.

[It has been observed that for a circle, the maximum number of pieces that can be produced by n cuts is $\dfrac{n^2 + n}{2} + 1$, but

for a crescent, the number increases to $\dfrac{n^2 + 3n}{2} + 1$. —M.G.]

Answer 102

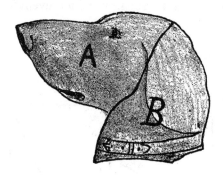

Answer 103

One person must travel 101,000 feet, or a little more than 19 miles, to gather the 100 potatoes!

Harry's best strategy is to select the 99th potato. Tom, being 2.04 percent faster, will take the first potato, Harry the second, Tom the third, and so on to the last. Tom is not fast enough to capture two adjacent potatoes. Harry will have to go 49,980 feet to bring in his 49 potatoes. During that same time, Tom will go 50,999.592 feet. Since he has to go 51,000 feet to bring in all 50 of his potatoes, Harry will win by less than half a foot!

Answer 104

In this simple example of "picture algebra" we find a capital illustration of the principles of substitution and the adding of like quantities to both sides of an equation without affecting the equilibrium, so to speak. It shows the truth of the axiom that things which are equal to the same things are equal to each other.

In the first equation we see that a top and three cubes equal twelve marbles. In the second equation a top alone equals a cube and eight marbles. Now let us add three cubes to each platform of the second scales. Since adding equal quantities to both sides will not affect the balance, we still have an equation. But now the left platform of the scales is identical with the left platform of the scales above it. We therefore must conclude that the two right platforms are also equal, namely, that four cubes and eight marbles must equal twelve marbles. Four cubes must therefore weigh the same as four marbles. In short, a cube and a marble weigh the same. The second picture tells us that a top balances with a cube and eight marbles, so we substitute a marble for the cube and find that the top is equal in weight to nine marbles.

Answer 105

In the octamal system 1906 is written 3562, which represents two units, six 8's, five 64's and three 512's. The simple procedure for arriving at this number is first to divide 1906 by 512 to obtain 3. The remainder, 370, is then divided by 64 to obtain 5. The remainder, 50, is divided by 8 to get 6, and the final remainder of 2 is of course the last digit of the answer. Had we wished to convert 1906 to the septamal system we would have followed a similar procedure, dividing by the successive multiples of 7.

Answer 106

Nine hundred picknickers started for the picnic in 100 wagons, 9 to a wagon.

Answer 107

Top Floor			Second Floor		
1	5	1	1	2	1
5		5	2		2
1	5	1	1	2	1

After the nine were carried off, the rest were arranged as follows:

Top Floor			Second Floor		
3	2	3	1	1	1
1		1	1		2
4	1	3	1	1	1

Answer 108

The number at the end of each paragraph denotes the number of manipulations in that paragraph.

The hhd. contains 63 gall. water, and the barrel 31½ gall. wine. Fill the three 10-gall. bottles with wine, pouring remaining 1½ gall. into 2-gall. measure, thus emptying barrel (4).

By means of the 4-gall. measure fill barrel from hhd., eventually leaving ½ gall. in 4-gall. measure. Give this ½ gall. to camel No. 1. By means of 4-gall. measure return 28 gall. of water from barrel to hhd. Pour 1½ gall. wine from 2-gall. measure into 4-gall. measure. Pour 2 gall. water from barrel into 2-gall. measure and return to hhd. Draw off remaining 1½ gall. water from barrel into 2-gall. measure and give this to camel No. 2. Pour 1½ gall. wine from 4-gall. measure into 2-gall. measure (37).

Repeat the whole of the operations in last paragraph eleven more times, so that six camels shall have each received two ½-gall. drinks, and another six camels two 1½-gall. drinks. But on the tenth and eleventh repetition, instead of returning the 2 gall. to hhd., deliver them to any two camels who have already received two ½ gall. only. Eight camels have now received 3 gall. each, and four camels 1 gall. each, and there will be 35 gall. water in hhd. (407).

Fill barrel from hogshead, using 4-gall. measure and give ½ gall. over to camel No. 13. Draw 3 gall. from hogshead into 4-gall. measure (18).

Return all wine to hogshead. Empty barrel into three 10-gall. bottles, and draw remaining 1½ gall. into 2-gall. measure. Return contents of three bottles to barrel, and pour 1½ gall. from 2-gall. measure into bottle No. 1 (12).

Fill the 2-gall. measure from 4 gall., leaving 1 gall. in 4 gall. Fill barrel from 2-gall. measure, and give remaining ½ gall. to camel No. 13. Give five camels 2 gall. each, all the camels having now been served (13).

Fill the two empty bottles from barrel, and draw remaining 1½ gall. into bottle No. 1. Return contents of bottles Nos. 2 and 3 to barrel (5).

Pour 1 gall. from 4-gall. measure into No. 2 bottle. Put 6 gall. wine in bottle No. 3, using 2-gall. and 4-gall. measures. Empty the 1 gall. from bottle No. 2 into 4-gall. measure, and fill up that measure with wine from bottle No. 3. Pour contents of 4-gall. measure into bottle No. 2. Draw 2 gall. water from barrel and put into bottle No. 2 (10).

The thirteen camels have now each received 3 gall. of water, one of the 10-gall. bottles contains 3 gall. of water, another 3 gall. of wine, and the third 3 gall. of wine and 3 gall. of water mixed. The hogshead contains 25½ gall. of wine, and the barrel 18 gall. of water. Total number of manipulations: 506.

[In an interview published in *The Strand* magazine, April, 1926, Henry Dudeney, England's great puzzlist, disclosed that Loyd once appealed to him for help on this problem. Loyd had offered cash prizes to his readers for the best solution and was anxious to avoid giving them by having an answer of his own that topped all those received. Dudeney worked out a solution in 521 moves which he later reduced to the 506 given above. This did the trick and Loyd always claimed that Dudeney had saved him thousands of dollars. —M.G.]

Answer 109

Many good mathematicians fell into the error of attempting to solve this on the basis of there being 24 starting points and the same number of endings. They reasoned that the square of 24, viz: 576 different ways, would be the correct answer. They overlooked the branch routes which give exactly

252 ways of reaching the center, C, and as there are just as
many ways of getting back out to the w's, the square of 252
gives the correct answer—63,504 different ways.

Answer 110

There would certainly have been a battle royal in the
Siamese aquarium had there been as many fishes in that fight
as I have received answers to this problem, and all maintain-
ing such different views!

For clearness and simplicity, I am inclined to accept the following decision of the time-keeper as being correct:

Three of the little fish paired off with each of three big fish,
engaging their attention while the other four little fighters
polished off the fourth big one in just three minutes. Then five
little fellows tackled one big fish and killed him in 2 minutes
and 24 seconds, while the other little ones were battling with
the other big ones.

It is evident that if the remaining two groups had been
assisted by one more fighter they would all have finished in the
same time, so there is only sufficient resistance left in each of
the big ones to call for the attention of a little fish for 2 minutes and 24 seconds. Therefore if seven now attack instead of
one, they would do it in one-seventh of that time, or 20 and
4/7 of a second.

In dividing the little fish forces against the remaining two
big ones—one would be attacked by seven and the other by six
—the last fish at the end of the 20 and 4/7 seconds would still
require the punishment which one little one could administer
in that time. The whole thirteen little fellows, concentrating
their attack, would give the fish his quietus in one-thirteenth
that time, or 1 and 53/91 seconds.

Adding up the totals of the time given in the several rounds
—3 minutes, 2 minutes and 24 seconds, 20 and 4/7 seconds,
and 1 and 53/91 seconds, we have 5 minutes, 46 and 2/13 seconds as the entire time consumed in the battle.

Answer 111

According to the information given, one round-holed coin
is worth 15/11 of a bit, one square-holed coin is worth 16/11

of a bit, and one triangular-holed coin is worth 17/11 of a bit. The pup, worth 11 bits, could therefore be bought with one square-holed coin and seven round-holed coins.

Answer *112*

The cheese is divided in two pieces by one cut, 4 by the second, 8 by the third, 15 by the fourth, 26 by the fifth, and 42 by the sixth.

[These numbers indicate the maximum number of pieces that can be produced by each successive cut of a convex solid. From this series it is not difficult to derive the following cubic equation, expressing the functional relation of the maximum number of pieces to the number of cuts (n) :

$$\frac{n^3 + 5n}{6} + 1 = \text{number of pieces}$$

—M.G.]

Answer *113*

The probability that not one of the six men will get his own hat is 265/720.

[This is arrived at as follows. The number of ways that n hats can be taken at random without a person getting his own hat is:

$$n! \left(1 - \frac{1}{1!} + \frac{1}{2!} - \frac{1}{3!} + \frac{1}{4!} \dots \pm \frac{1}{n!}\right)$$

This over factorial n (the total number of ways the hats can be selected) gives the answer. As n increases, the answer approaches closer and closer to $1/e$ as a limit, thus providing a curious empirical technique for calculating the transcendental number e. See W. Rouse Ball's *Mathematical Recreations*, current edition, p. 46, for an analysis of this problem, with application to similar questions involving the matching of playing cards in two shuffled packs.—M.G.]

Answer *114*

The accompanying diagram shows the one correct way of picketing the cornfield with eight crows so that every bird has an unobstructed view of all the others, and so that there are no two birds in the same row or diagonal. It also is impossible for the hunter to discover any standpoint from which he might get a line-shot on three birds.

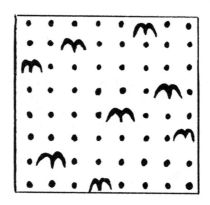

Answer 115

The "pretty trick" turns on the fact that two niches in the border of the center hole are obscured by the prisoner's head! The following diagrams show how the board is cut.

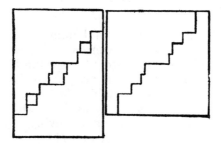

Answer 116

Butcher Boy cost $264 and was sold at $295.68, a 12 percent profit. The other horse cost $220 and was sold for $198, a 10 percent loss. Total cost, $484; total received, $493.68, making a 2 percent profit on the whole.

Answer 117

The scissors are removed from the cord by working the looped end back along the double cord. First through the left ring, then the right ring, then left, then right. Now pass the loop over the entire pair of scissors and it will come free unless you have produced an unfortunate tangle by twisting the cord.

SELECTED REFERENCES

Chess Strategy: a Treatise upon the Art of Problem Composition, by Sam Loyd, 1878. Privately published: Elizabeth, N. J. A collection of about 500 of Loyd's chess problems.

Sam Loyd and His Chess Problems, by Alain C. White, 1913. Whitehead and Miller: Leeds, England. A major source of biographical information on Loyd. (Dover Reprint)

Sam Loyd's Puzzles: a Book for Children, edited by Sam Loyd II, 1912. David McKay: Philadelphia.

Sam Loyd's Cyclopedia of 5000 Puzzles, Tricks, and Conundrums, edited by Sam Loyd II, 1914. The Lamb Publishing Company: New York.

Sam Loyd's Picture Puzzles, edited by Sam Loyd II, 1924. Privately printed: New York.

Sam Loyd and His Puzzles, edited by Sam Loyd II, 1928, Barse and Company: New York.

"The Prince of Puzzle Makers," by George C. Bain. *The Strand Magazine,* December, 1907.

"My Fifty Years in Puzzleland," by Walter P. Eaton. *Delineator,* April, 1911.

"Geometrical Vanishes," Chapters 7 and 8, *Mathematics, Magic, and Mystery,* by Martin Gardner, 1956. Dover Publications: New York. A detailed discussion of Loyd's "Get off the Earth" puzzle and related paradoxes.

"Mathematical Games," by Martin Gardner. *Scientific American,* August, 1957, On Sam Loyd and his puzzles, with reproductions of Loyd's original "Trick Donkeys" and "Teddy and the Lions" puzzles.

A CATALOG OF SELECTED DOVER
BOOKS IN ALL FIELDS OF INTEREST

DRAWINGS OF REMBRANDT, edited by Seymour Slive. Updated Lippmann, Hofstede de Groot edition, with definitive scholarly apparatus. All portraits, biblical sketches, landscapes, nudes. Oriental figures, classical studies, together with selection of work by followers. 550 illustrations. Total of 630pp. 9⅛ × 12¼.
21485-0, 21486-9 Pa., Two-vol. set $25.00

GHOST AND HORROR STORIES OF AMBROSE BIERCE, Ambrose Bierce. 24 tales vividly imagined, strangely prophetic, and decades ahead of their time in technical skill: "The Damned Thing," "An Inhabitant of Carcosa," "The Eyes of the Panther," "Moxon's Master," and 20 more. 199pp. 5⅜ × 8½. 20767-6 Pa. $3.95

ETHICAL WRITINGS OF MAIMONIDES, Maimonides. Most significant ethical works of great medieval sage, newly translated for utmost precision, readability. Laws Concerning Character Traits, Eight Chapters, more. 192pp. 5⅜ × 8½.
24522-5 Pa. $4.50

THE EXPLORATION OF THE COLORADO RIVER AND ITS CANYONS, J. W. Powell. Full text of Powell's 1,000-mile expedition down the fabled Colorado in 1869. Superb account of terrain, geology, vegetation, Indians, famine, mutiny, treacherous rapids, mighty canyons, during exploration of last unknown part of continental U.S. 400pp. 5⅜ × 8½. 20094-9 Pa. $6.95

HISTORY OF PHILOSOPHY, Julián Marías. Clearest one-volume history on the market. Every major philosopher and dozens of others, to Existentialism and later. 505pp. 5⅜ × 8½. 21739-6 Pa. $8.50

ALL ABOUT LIGHTNING, Martin A. Uman. Highly readable non-technical survey of nature and causes of lightning, thunderstorms, ball lightning, St. Elmo's Fire, much more. Illustrated. 192pp. 5⅜ × 8½. 25237-X Pa. $5.95

SAILING ALONE AROUND THE WORLD, Captain Joshua Slocum. First man to sail around the world, alone, in small boat. One of great feats of seamanship told in delightful manner. 67 illustrations. 294pp. 5⅜ × 8½. 20326-3 Pa. $4.95

LETTERS AND NOTES ON THE MANNERS, CUSTOMS AND CONDITIONS OF THE NORTH AMERICAN INDIANS, George Catlin. Classic account of life among Plains Indians: ceremonies, hunt, warfare, etc. 312 plates. 572pp. of text. 6⅛ × 9¼. 22118-0, 22119-9 Pa. Two-vol. set $15.90

ALASKA: The Harriman Expedition, 1899, John Burroughs, John Muir, et al. Informative, engrossing accounts of two-month, 9,000-mile expedition. Native peoples, wildlife, forests, geography, salmon industry, glaciers, more. Profusely illustrated. 240 black-and-white line drawings. 124 black-and-white photographs. 3 maps. Index. 576pp. 5⅜ × 8½. 25109-8 Pa. $11.95

A CONCISE HISTORY OF PHOTOGRAPHY: Third Revised Edition, Helmut Gernsheim. Best one-volume history—camera obscura, photochemistry, daguerreotypes, evolution of cameras, film, more. Also artistic aspects—landscape, portraits, fine art, etc. 281 black-and-white photographs. 26 in color. 176pp. 8⅜ × 11¼. 25128-4 Pa. $12.95

THE DORÉ BIBLE ILLUSTRATIONS, Gustave Doré. 241 detailed plates from the Bible: the Creation scenes, Adam and Eve, Flood, Babylon, battle sequences, life of Jesus, etc. Each plate is accompanied by the verses from the King James version of the Bible. 241pp. 9 × 12. 23004-X Pa. $8.95

HUGGER-MUGGER IN THE LOUVRE, Elliot Paul. Second Homer Evans mystery-comedy. Theft at the Louvre involves sleuth in hilarious, madcap caper. "A knockout."—Books. 336pp. 5⅜ × 8½. 25185-3 Pa. $5.95

FLATLAND, E. A. Abbott. Intriguing and enormously popular science-fiction classic explores the complexities of trying to survive as a two-dimensional being in a three-dimensional world. Amusingly illustrated by the author. 16 illustrations. 103pp. 5⅜ × 8½. 20001-9 Pa. $2.25

THE HISTORY OF THE LEWIS AND CLARK EXPEDITION, Meriwether Lewis and William Clark, edited by Elliott Coues. Classic edition of Lewis and Clark's day-by-day journals that later became the basis for U.S. claims to Oregon and the West. Accurate and invaluable geographical, botanical, biological, meteorological and anthropological material. Total of 1,508pp. 5⅜ × 8½.
21268-8, 21269-6, 21270-X Pa. Three-vol. set $25.50

LANGUAGE, TRUTH AND LOGIC, Alfred J. Ayer. Famous, clear introduction to Vienna, Cambridge schools of Logical Positivism. Role of philosophy, elimination of metaphysics, nature of analysis, etc. 160pp. 5⅜ × 8½. (Available in U.S. and Canada only) 20010-8 Pa. $2.95

MATHEMATICS FOR THE NONMATHEMATICIAN, Morris Kline. Detailed, college-level treatment of mathematics in cultural and historical context, with numerous exercises. For liberal arts students. Preface. Recommended Reading Lists. Tables. Index. Numerous black-and-white figures. xvi + 641pp. 5⅜ × 8½.
24823-2 Pa. $11.95

28 SCIENCE FICTION STORIES, H. G. Wells. Novels, *Star Begotten* and *Men Like Gods,* plus 26 short stories: "Empire of the Ants," "A Story of the Stone Age," "The Stolen Bacillus," "In the Abyss," etc. 915pp. 5⅜ × 8½. (Available in U.S. only)
20265-8 Cloth. $10.95

HANDBOOK OF PICTORIAL SYMBOLS, Rudolph Modley. 3,250 signs and symbols, many systems in full; official or heavy commercial use. Arranged by subject. Most in Pictorial Archive series. 143pp. 8⅛ × 11. 23357-X Pa. $5.95

INCIDENTS OF TRAVEL IN YUCATAN, John L. Stephens. Classic (1843) exploration of jungles of Yucatan, looking for evidences of Maya civilization. Travel adventures, Mexican and Indian culture, etc. Total of 669pp. 5⅜ × 8½.
20926-1, 20927-X Pa., Two-vol. set $9.90

DEGAS: An Intimate Portrait, Ambroise Vollard. Charming, anecdotal memoir by famous art dealer of one of the greatest 19th-century French painters. 14 black-and-white illustrations. Introduction by Harold L. Van Doren. 96pp. 5⅜ × 8½.
25131-4 Pa. $3.95

PERSONAL NARRATIVE OF A PILGRIMAGE TO ALMANDINAH AND MECCAH, Richard Burton. Great travel classic by remarkably colorful personality. Burton, disguised as a Moroccan, visited sacred shrines of Islam, narrowly escaping death. 47 illustrations. 959pp. 5⅜ × 8½. 21217-3, 21218-1 Pa., Two-vol. set $17.90

PHRASE AND WORD ORIGINS, A. H. Holt. Entertaining, reliable, modern study of more than 1,200 colorful words, phrases, origins and histories. Much unexpected information. 254pp. 5⅜ × 8½.
20758-7 Pa. $5.95

THE RED THUMB MARK, R. Austin Freeman. In this first Dr. Thorndyke case, the great scientific detective draws fascinating conclusions from the nature of a single fingerprint. Exciting story, authentic science. 320pp. 5⅜ × 8½. (Available in U.S. only)
25210-8 Pa. $5.95

AN EGYPTIAN HIEROGLYPHIC DICTIONARY, E. A. Wallis Budge. Monumental work containing about 25,000 words or terms that occur in texts ranging from 3000 B.C. to 600 A.D. Each entry consists of a transliteration of the word, the word in hieroglyphs, and the meaning in English. 1,314pp. 6⅜ × 10.
23615-3, 23616-1 Pa., Two-vol. set $27.90

THE COMPLEAT STRATEGYST: Being a Primer on the Theory of Games of Strategy, J. D. Williams. Highly entertaining classic describes, with many illustrated examples, how to select best strategies in conflict situations. Prefaces. Appendices. xvi + 268pp. 5⅜ × 8½.
25101-2 Pa. $5.95

THE ROAD TO OZ, L. Frank Baum. Dorothy meets the Shaggy Man, little Button-Bright and the Rainbow's beautiful daughter in this delightful trip to the magical Land of Oz. 272pp. 5⅜ × 8.
25208-6 Pa. $4.95

POINT AND LINE TO PLANE, Wassily Kandinsky. Seminal exposition of role of point, line, other elements in non-objective painting. Essential to understanding 20th-century art. 127 illustrations. 192pp. 6½ × 9¼.
23808-3 Pa. $4.50

LADY ANNA, Anthony Trollope. Moving chronicle of Countess Lovel's bitter struggle to win for herself and daughter Anna their rightful rank and fortune—perhaps at cost of sanity itself. 384pp. 5⅜ × 8½.
24669-8 Pa. $6.95

EGYPTIAN MAGIC, E. A. Wallis Budge. Sums up all that is known about magic in Ancient Egypt: the role of magic in controlling the gods, powerful amulets that warded off evil spirits, scarabs of immortality, use of wax images, formulas and spells, the secret name, much more. 253pp. 5⅜ × 8½.
22681-6 Pa. $4.50

THE DANCE OF SIVA, Ananda Coomaraswamy. Preeminent authority unfolds the vast metaphysic of India: the revelation of her art, conception of the universe, social organization, etc. 27 reproductions of art masterpieces. 192pp. 5⅜ × 8½.
24817-8 Pa. $5.95

CHRISTMAS CUSTOMS AND TRADITIONS, Clement A. Miles. Origin, evolution, significance of religious, secular practices. Caroling, gifts, yule logs, much more. Full, scholarly yet fascinating; non-sectarian. 400pp. 5⅜ × 8½.
23354-5 Pa. $6.50

THE HUMAN FIGURE IN MOTION, Eadweard Muybridge. More than 4,500 stopped-action photos, in action series, showing undraped men, women, children jumping, lying down, throwing, sitting, wrestling, carrying, etc. 390pp. 7⅞ × 10⅝.
20204-6 Cloth. $19.95

THE MAN WHO WAS THURSDAY, Gilbert Keith Chesterton. Witty, fast-paced novel about a club of anarchists in turn-of-the-century London. Brilliant social, religious, philosophical speculations. 128pp. 5⅜ × 8½. 25121-7 Pa. $3.95

A CEZANNE SKETCHBOOK: Figures, Portraits, Landscapes and Still Lifes, Paul Cezanne. Great artist experiments with tonal effects, light, mass, other qualities in over 100 drawings. A revealing view of developing master painter, precursor of Cubism. 102 black-and-white illustrations. 144pp. 8¾ × 6⅜. 24790-2 Pa. $5.95

AN ENCYCLOPEDIA OF BATTLES: Accounts of Over 1,560 Battles from 1479 B.C. to the Present, David Eggenberger. Presents essential details of every major battle in recorded history, from the first battle of Megiddo in 1479 B.C. to Grenada in 1984. List of Battle Maps. New Appendix covering the years 1967–1984. Index. 99 illustrations. 544pp. 6½ × 9¼. 24913-1 Pa. $14.95

AN ETYMOLOGICAL DICTIONARY OF MODERN ENGLISH, Ernest Weekley. Richest, fullest work, by foremost British lexicographer. Detailed word histories. Inexhaustible. Total of 856pp. 6½ × 9¼.
21873-2, 21874-0 Pa., Two-vol. set $17.00

WEBSTER'S AMERICAN MILITARY BIOGRAPHIES, edited by Robert McHenry. Over 1,000 figures who shaped 3 centuries of American military history. Detailed biographies of Nathan Hale, Douglas MacArthur, Mary Hallaren, others. Chronologies of engagements, more. Introduction. Addenda. 1,033 entries in alphabetical order. xi + 548pp. 6½ × 9¼. (Available in U.S. only)
24758-9 Pa. $11.95

LIFE IN ANCIENT EGYPT, Adolf Erman. Detailed older account, with much not in more recent books: domestic life, religion, magic, medicine, commerce, and whatever else needed for complete picture. Many illustrations. 597pp. 5⅜ × 8½.
22632-8 Pa. $8.95

HISTORIC COSTUME IN PICTURES, Braun & Schneider. Over 1,450 costumed figures shown, covering a wide variety of peoples: kings, emperors, nobles, priests, servants, soldiers, scholars, townsfolk, peasants, merchants, courtiers, cavaliers, and more. 256pp. 8⅜ × 11¼. 23150-X Pa. $7.95

THE NOTEBOOKS OF LEONARDO DA VINCI, edited by J. P. Richter. Extracts from manuscripts reveal great genius; on painting, sculpture, anatomy, sciences, geography, etc. Both Italian and English. 186 ms. pages reproduced, plus 500 additional drawings, including studies for *Last Supper, Sforza* monument, etc. 860pp. 7⅞ × 10¾. (Available in U.S. only) 22572-0, 22573-9 Pa., Two-vol. set $25.90

SIR HARRY HOTSPUR OF HUMBLETHWAITE, Anthony Trollope. Incisive, unconventional psychological study of a conflict between a wealthy baronet, his idealistic daughter, and their scapegrace cousin. The 1870 novel in its first inexpensive edition in years. 250pp. 5⅜ × 8½. 24953-0 Pa. $5.95

LASERS AND HOLOGRAPHY, Winston E. Kock. Sound introduction to burgeoning field, expanded (1981) for second edition. Wave patterns, coherence, lasers, diffraction, zone plates, properties of holograms, recent advances. 84 illustrations. 160pp. 5⅜ × 8¼. (Except in United Kingdom) 24041-X Pa. $3.50

INTRODUCTION TO ARTIFICIAL INTELLIGENCE: SECOND, EN-LARGED EDITION, Philip C. Jackson, Jr. Comprehensive survey of artificial intelligence—the study of how machines (computers) can be made to act intelli-gently. Includes introductory and advanced material. Extensive notes updating the main text. 132 black-and-white illustrations. 512pp. 5⅜ × 8½. 24864-X Pa. $8.95

HISTORY OF INDIAN AND INDONESIAN ART, Ananda K. Coomaraswamy. Over 400 illustrations illuminate classic study of Indian art from earliest Harappa finds to early 20th century. Provides philosophical, religious and social insights. 304pp. 6⅜ × 9⅜. 25005-9 Pa. $8.95

THE GOLEM, Gustav Meyrink. Most famous supernatural novel in modern European literature, set in Ghetto of Old Prague around 1890. Compelling story of mystical experiences, strange transformations, profound terror. 13 black-and-white illustrations. 224pp. 5⅜ × 8½. (Available in U.S. only) 25025-3 Pa. $5.95

ARMADALE, Wilkie Collins. Third great mystery novel by the author of *The Woman in White* and *The Moonstone*. Original magazine version with 40 illustrations. 597pp. 5⅜ × 8½. 23429-0 Pa. $9.95

PICTORIAL ENCYCLOPEDIA OF HISTORIC ARCHITECTURAL PLANS, DETAILS AND ELEMENTS: With 1,880 Line Drawings of Arches, Domes, Doorways, Facades, Gables, Windows, etc., John Theodore Haneman. Sourcebook of inspiration for architects, designers, others. Bibliography. Captions. 141pp. 9 × 12. 24605-1 Pa. $6.95

BENCHLEY LOST AND FOUND, Robert Benchley. Finest humor from early 30's, about pet peeves, child psychologists, post office and others. Mostly unavailable elsewhere. 73 illustrations by Peter Arno and others. 183pp. 5⅜ × 8½. 22410-4 Pa. $3.95

ERTÉ GRAPHICS, Erté. Collection of striking color graphics: *Seasons, Alphabet, Numerals, Aces* and *Precious Stones*. 50 plates, including 4 on covers. 48pp. 9⅜ × 12¼. 23580-7 Pa. $6.95

THE JOURNAL OF HENRY D. THOREAU, edited by Bradford Torrey, F. H. Allen. Complete reprinting of 14 volumes, 1837–61, over two million words; the sourcebooks for *Walden*, etc. Definitive. All original sketches, plus 75 photographs. 1,804pp. 8½ × 12¼. 20312-3, 20313-1 Cloth., Two-vol. set $80.00

CASTLES: THEIR CONSTRUCTION AND HISTORY, Sidney Toy. Traces castle development from ancient roots. Nearly 200 photographs and drawings illustrate moats, keeps, baileys, many other features. Caernarvon, Dover Castles, Hadrian's Wall, Tower of London, dozens more. 256pp. 5⅜ × 8¼. 24898-4 Pa. $5.95

AMERICAN CLIPPER SHIPS: 1833-1858, Octavius T. Howe & Frederick C. Matthews. Fully-illustrated, encyclopedic review of 352 clipper ships from the period of America's greatest maritime supremacy. Introduction. 109 halftones. 5 black-and-white line illustrations. Index. Total of 928pp. 5⅜ × 8½.
25115-2, 25116-0 Pa., Two-vol. set $17.90

TOWARDS A NEW ARCHITECTURE, Le Corbusier. Pioneering manifesto by great architect, near legendary founder of "International School." Technical and aesthetic theories, views on industry, economics, relation of form to function, "mass-production spirit," much more. Profusely illustrated. Unabridged translation of 13th French edition. Introduction by Frederick Etchells. 320pp. 6⅛ × 9¼.
(Available in U.S. only)
25023-7 Pa. $8.95

THE BOOK OF KELLS, edited by Blanche Cirker. Inexpensive collection of 32 full-color, full-page plates from the greatest illuminated manuscript of the Middle Ages, painstakingly reproduced from rare facsimile edition. Publisher's Note. Captions. 32pp. 9⅜ × 12¼.
24345-1 Pa. $4.95

BEST SCIENCE FICTION STORIES OF H. G. WELLS, H. G. Wells. Full novel *The Invisible Man*, plus 17 short stories: "The Crystal Egg," "Aepyornis Island," "The Strange Orchid," etc. 303pp. 5⅜ × 8½. (Available in U.S. only)
21531-8 Pa. $4.95

AMERICAN SAILING SHIPS: Their Plans and History, Charles G. Davis. Photos, construction details of schooners, frigates, clippers, other sailcraft of 18th to early 20th centuries—plus entertaining discourse on design, rigging, nautical lore, much more. 137 black-and-white illustrations. 240pp. 6⅛ × 9¼.
24658-2 Pa. $5.95

ENTERTAINING MATHEMATICAL PUZZLES, Martin Gardner. Selection of author's favorite conundrums involving arithmetic, money, speed, etc., with lively commentary. Complete solutions. 112pp. 5⅜ × 8½.
25211-6 Pa. $2.95

THE WILL TO BELIEVE, HUMAN IMMORTALITY, William James. Two books bound together. Effect of irrational on logical, and arguments for human immortality. 402pp. 5⅜ × 8½.
20291-7 Pa. $7.50

THE HAUNTED MONASTERY and THE CHINESE MAZE MURDERS, Robert Van Gulik. 2 full novels by Van Gulik continue adventures of Judge Dee and his companions. An evil Taoist monastery, seemingly supernatural events; overgrown topiary maze that hides strange crimes. Set in 7th-century China. 27 illustrations. 328pp. 5⅜ × 8½.
23502-5 Pa. $5.95

CELEBRATED CASES OF JUDGE DEE (DEE GOONG AN), translated by Robert Van Gulik. Authentic 18th-century Chinese detective novel; Dee and associates solve three interlocked cases. Led to Van Gulik's own stories with same characters. Extensive introduction. 9 illustrations. 237pp. 5⅜ × 8½.
23337-5 Pa. $4.95

Prices subject to change without notice.
Available at your book dealer or write for free catalog to Dept. GI, Dover Publications, Inc., 31 East 2nd St., Mineola, N.Y. 11501. Dover publishes more than 175 books each year on science, elementary and advanced mathematics, biology, music, art, literary history, social sciences and other areas.

9